SENSE OF
SOURCE

AN INDUSTRY OF BEAUTY AND PAIN

Robert McLaughlin

Copyright © 2024 by Robert McLaughlin.

All rights reserved. No part of this book may be reproduced in any written, electronic, recording, or photocopying without written permission of the publisher or author. The exception would be in the case of brief quotations embodied on the pages where the publisher or author specifically grants permission.

This book is dedicated to my wife, Kristine, whose unwavering support has been a cornerstone in my life. She has made numerous sacrifices, transitioning from a successful career to raising our children, frequently shouldering the responsibilities of parenthood alone and working tirelessly at companies we owned or worked at to help me be successful. I am forever thankful for all her support.

To my children Brian and Emily, you embody the greatest measure of success in my life and your stories are now under way.

Introduction

If you look closely you can get a Sense of Source in any person, company, or industry and capture a better understanding of how the products or services you buy came to be. My company Florida Fresh Events is a floral company that came to exist over a 40 year career in the floral and event industry.

There is a symbiotic relationship between beauty and pain. A rose and the floral industry provide a perfect example of this relationship. I hope you will enjoy reading about my journey in this industry and how my company grew into one of the leading event decor companies in Central Florida. Orlando is the busiest city in the country for events with its beautiful weather year round and the best theme parks in the world. Floral decor is mainly a perishable industry, always presented with challenges other industries do not face, but the results for me have been well worth the time, effort, and energy.

My journey began 40 years ago, taking me from greenhouses in Central Florida to farms in Central and South America to the boardrooms of San Francisco and back to theme parks in Central Florida. With this book, I hope to provide an inside look into the floral and event industry and the changes it has experienced since the 1980s. As one of the few books about this complex industry, I will share how it has evolved from a locally grown industry to a global marketplace with some of the most extreme examples of supply and demand theory.

Whether you are an event company, grower, retailer, wholesaler, or simply a lover of one of nature's best and most colorful gifts, I invite you to take a journey into my personal history to discover how it shaped my role in the industry. My career has taken me into many dangerous back alleyways in places like Bogota and Medellin, Colombia. I've overseen major agricultural operations, set up floral programs in national chain retailers, and run into DEA and CIA operatives among many other trials and adventures. In my book you might find the floral industry is not all roses – literally and figuratively – and may see the next bouquet of flowers you give or receive in a whole new way.

Whatever you take from this book, I hope it is positive and I thank you for reading!

--Robert

Table of Contents

CHAPTER 1: Welcome to the Jungle	7
CHAPTER 2: Flowers in Colombia	9
CHAPTER 3: Growers, Guerrillas, and Really Bad Coffee	13
CHAPTER 4: UNINTENTIONAL DRUG WAR VIOLENCE EXPERIENCES	18
CHAPTER 5: My Beginning is a Look Back	24
CHAPTER 6 : Dumb Decisions Somehow Equaled Promotions	27
CHAPTER 7: Wise Guys and One Nasty Hurricane	32
CHAPTER 8: Moving to Ecuador	37
CHAPTER 9: Business Expansions, Ethical Crises, and Corrupt Politicians	44
CHAPTER 10: Importing Flowers + Concealed Carry = Getting Stopped By Florida Drug Enforcement Officers	51
CHAPTER 11: The Commercial and Personal Pitfalls of a Perishable Industry	57
CHAPTER 12: Working With the 'Marts', New Deals, and Trimming Company Fat	66
CHAPTER 13: Real Estate, Helping Other Floral Businesses, Lots of Traveling and a Car Chase	76
CHAPTER 14: The Good CEO Fight and Why Organic isn't Always	88
CHAPTER 15: Haiti and Goodwill	102
CHAPTER 16: New Consulting Projects and High Altitudes	111
CHAPTER 17: Climbing to New Heights - Mexico	118
CHAPTER 18: COVID and Migration to Orlando	123

CHAPTER ONE: Welcome to the Jungle

In 2024, the floral industry is estimated to be a $57.4 billion dollar a year industry worldwide. Eighty percent of the cut flowers sold in the United States come from Colombia and Ecuador.

The floriculture industry in Colombia began in the late 1970s. It came about not only by inexpensive labor and excellent growing conditions but also, in the beginning, by the United States' war on marijuana production. The U.S. war on drugs brought U.S. aid to Colombia to support the growing of flowers instead of marijuana. Ironically some 50 years later the U.S. has determined marijuana is not only okay for medical use but also for recreational enjoyment. The war against drugs in Colombia has resulted in a 40-year civil war, costing tens of thousands of lives from violence and the adverse health effects from the overspray of Agent Orange-like defoliants used to kill off illicit drug crops. Almost everyone I know in Colombia has a friend or family member who has been killed or injured by the war on drugs waged by the United States. Flowers are right in the middle of this decades long battle of beauty and pain.

Since the emergence of South American flowers, we have seen U.S. growers go out of business at an alarming rate with multigenerational farmers put out of their homes and their land sold to developers. I believe within 10 years after marijuana is finally legalized at the federal level, we will see

Colombian growers of marijuana put U.S. marijuana growers out of business coming full circle to where we were in the 1970s with much of the world's marijuana grown in Colombia and Ecuador. It's been a painful 50 years of politicians playing God with people's lives and brings credence to the saying that "history repeats itself."

My time in this industry started in 1984 working at a farm in the small town of Apopka, FL, just north of Orlando. Apopka is the self-proclaimed indoor foliage capital of the world that at one time had hundreds of small to large greenhouse and shade cloth operations. I started with packing boxes and moved through the ranks to driving trucks and then to the sales of plants to local supermarkets.

CHAPTER TWO: Flowers in Colombia

Since I became a salesman to supermarkets of potted plants and hardgoods, it made sense that I start selling cut flowers as well. I didn't know much about them or where they came from but given my experience with potted plants, I knew I wanted to get closer to the source and cut out the middlemen. I looked over the first boxes that came to us from Miami importers and most of them had grower phone and fax numbers in Bogota and Medellin, Colombia.

At the time I couldn't have told you where Colombia was. We didn't have Google back then, so I hit the encyclopedia to see what I could learn about the country. I followed up my research with a trip to a bookstore for the *Fodor's Travel Guide* on Colombia. I was now as smart as the next guy about Columbia, or so I thought.

Soon after, I convinced my boss to invest in a fax machine. My work required communicating with growers in Colombia, which was problematic given I didn't speak Spanish, email did not exist, and long-distance calls were so expensive they were not worth the insane phone bills which followed. Telex machines had recently been replaced by fax machines, but our farm didn't have one. I purchased the fax machine and immediately started to fax every grower I had put in my Rolodex. The response wasn't great; most farms had operations in Miami or relationships with importers to handle their North American sales, so I decided to fly to Bogota to look in the local phone books for more numbers.

Once I booked the flight, I faxed every number I had to let the South American growers know I was in route and meant business. I couldn't believe how many replies I received because the growers were interested to see who was crazy enough to come to Colombia. It was a war zone in the late '80s and early '90s, with the infamous drug kingpin Pablo Escobar overseeing widespread killings that often played out on the streets of Medellin, Bogota, and Miami. It was a particularly dangerous time to be in any business that originated in Colombia and distributed out of Miami.

As a 20-year-old during the heyday of TV's *Miami Vice,* I was excited to visit Bogota, ignoring the obvious dangers it presented. My fellow workers called me "young and dumb," and I placed a running bet with one of my work mates that I wouldn't be killed on my trip. We kept going double or nothing when I returned alive but with Escobar bombing a passenger jet one year, the bet was rolling too much in his favor. I'm still winning that bet but as I grew older, got married, and had kids, the joke wasn't as funny anymore. It's one thing when you're a kid without responsibilities or spawn to protect. It's another when you're a full-blown adult with a family.

Anyway, back to how the growers perceived my first visit, especially since so few "gringos" visited Colombia during that time even if they were floral industry members. The Colombians who lived in Miami controlled the flower trade, traveling back and forth to their native country, but even they were fearful. Since our company was a "regional player" that provided blooms to supermarkets, I knew I wanted to avoid the middleman. I wanted to *be* the middleman, I saw no value or purpose in helping someone else strengthen his relationship with my customers.

What I did want was to see *where* the flowers were grown. Our company supplied floral departments throughout Winn Dixie in Florida and Kroger stores in Georgia and Tennessee with everything from plants to balloons, ribbons, and bows.

Flowers were in huge demand for supermarket floral at the time.

Like most flights into Bogota, my first one landed at night. I took a cab from the airport to my hotel. I had all of my hotel information written down so I could show the driver instead of attempting verbal communication in extremely broken Spanglish. I had the name of the hotel – the Bogota Plaza – as well as the street address and phone number in case I needed to make a call. Cell phones were nonexistent back then, so I had to share all of the hotel information I could with the driver because once he started asking questions – well, you get by now that speaking Spanish was not my strong suit.

As we were driving through Bogota, I was starting to feel dizzy from the exhaust. In an effort to make friendly conversation, I used gestures and words indicating the vehicle might have an exhaust leak. The cab driver chuckled and in broken English told me, "Welcome to Colombia," noting that Bogota itself had an "exhaust leak." At the time four million people lived in Bogota with at least three million cars, most of which were taxis. Some 10 years and six million people later, the government implemented the *Pica Placa* law where only cars with odd/even license plate numbers could drive during peak hours. Driving opportunities alternated by day, and it smells much fresher in Bogota now. Back then it smelled worse than the acid rains in Los Angeles, and after days of meetings my throat felt raw, my nostrils coated with black soot. It was no joke; this place was high in the Andean Mountains and the smog of the city undoubtedly caused respiratory problems and secondhand lung cancer for many people.

When arriving on the night flights, the city was a beautiful sight. Looking out the windows I could see hundreds of greenhouses all over the savanna lit up. Bogota grew a lot of chrysanthemums and gypsophila (Baby's Breath) which needed to be lit at night, so there were thousands of acres of lighted greenhouses visible on final approach into the El Dorado International Airport. Arriving for the first time at night, I had no real idea where I was or what the city surroundings looked like. At 4 a.m., I decided to have a look-see. I went down to the hotel lobby to ask where I could buy cigarettes. The man at the lobby counter took me to see another guy, and I was using my Spanglish quite well to communicate. The second guy told me to follow him and he would get me cigarettes. I followed him out a hotel side door down a narrow alleyway, wondering more and more if I was going to get mugged or killed. I had absolutely no idea, but I knew running back into the safety of my hotel would have made me look stupid. At 20-something years old, I would have rather died than look dumb.

The man took me to another building where the doorman had a carton of cigarettes behind his podium. He sold me a pack for who-knows-how-much-money, but at that juncture I had already experienced enough stress to obtain them, so I wasn't going to chicken out. The man relieved me of Colombian pesos in my open wallet and soon I was back off to my hotel with my cigs. It was an adventure that gave a whole new meaning to the "cigarettes are bad and can kill you" mantra. Thus, ended my first night in Bogota, and it was nothing compared to my future South American exploits.

CHAPTER THREE: Growers, Guerrillas, and Really Bad Coffee

After surviving my first day of visiting a few farms, one particular grower *insisted* on treating me to dinner at his Country Club. His driver picked me up at 8 p.m. to drive me outside of town where the club was located. It took about an hour to get there, and while the areas surrounding Bogota were not considered safe at night, my 20-year-old self-paid no mind to the danger. As we were having dinner, the lights went out in the entire club. It was pitch black and I sat there, sweating like a racehorse, wondering if I was about to be killed. I was reassured that electrical problems were common in Colombia and not to worry, but as I had watched my fair share of *Miami Vice,* I was 1,000 percent convinced something bad was about to "go down."

Since Colombia's electrical grid wasn't the greatest, the incident truly *was* common and after five to 10 minutes the room enjoyed illumination once more. Of course, when you're sweating it out preparing yourself for a shooting in which you are the target, it seems much longer, giving me plenty of time to think of the worst possible outcomes. My *absolute worst fear* was that the restaurant was about to be stormed by rebels and we would be taken hostage for ransom to further fund their war. There were many fears to be had in Colombia in those days beyond the well-known kidnappings and drug violence. I read a story about a U.S. backpacker in Colombia who chipped a tooth and went to a dentist somewhere in the countryside. He woke up the next day face down on the streets of Bogota where some kind people took him to the U.S. Embassy. His entire head was wrapped in gauze and tape. As they unwrapped his head, they found his eyes had been harvested and likely sold on the black market for transplants. Colombia, at the time, was well known as the place for eyes and kidneys and ironically organ trade was not illegal in Colombia.

The next day the grower invited me back to the country club to play golf, during which I learned just how far a ball could go at high altitude. Hitting the golf balls off a cliff to a lower fairway through the thin air – well, they certainly traveled farther than any previous small ball I had smacked with a club. I'm from Florida after all, which is about as flat as it gets. The Bogota Country Club was a walking course and at the higher altitude it was also a good acclimatizing exercise for a young man from Florida.

Even though I was enjoying my time in Bogota, Colombia, during the '80s and even the '90s it was the kidnapping capital of the world. Someone suggested I procure kidnapping insurance, a type of coverage other importers and exporters frequently bought. Drug wars in the South American country had already been raging for 10 years, and kidnapping provided guerrilla groups with opportunities to make serious ransom or earn organ harvesting money. Kidnapping and ransoms became a way of life there, causing many companies to purchase coverage for their employees.

A friend of mine was kidnapped with his wife after having dinner outside the city. I have known several growers who were kidnapped, one of which spent almost two years in a hole deep in the jungle before securing his release with a large cash payment. While he returned to his family, he was never the same and had to leave the country and the floral industry. A good friend of mine, now living in Miami, had his housekeeper's cousin attempt to kidnap his children from their school. It was a terrifying way to live.

I was stopped a few times outside the city of Colombia by armed men who pretended to be national police. They took my passport or identification card and ran it through a laptop or book of papers on the hood of a pickup truck which vaguely resembled a police vehicle. Once, a grower I was riding with told me those men were *not* police, but members of the FARC (translated - Revolutionary Armed Forces of Colombia) who were running IDs to see if I and others like me had kidnapping insurance or met organ harvesting demands. It pretty much ended my interest in having that type of insurance.

By the start of the next decade I was still visiting farms in Bogota and the surrounding areas, where I had to radio ahead to see if there was guerrilla activity in the area in order to plan a visit. Sometimes I had to wait a day or two to visit specific growers until it was clear to go.

For guerrilla and general security reasons, I would hire a car and driver to take me to the Colombian farms where I had meetings. A decade later, a farm wouldn't *think* of allowing me to take a car; they always picked me up at the hotel. While Escobar was still alive, it wasn't safe for anyone to travel in the area so growers weren't making extra trips or sending cars. I often spent entire days going from farm to farm, working with non-English speaking drivers to find our way to each meeting in the days before GPS. At the end of those days trekking down dirt or pothole-filled roads in and around Bogota I would get back to the hotel, smack the dust off my pants and blow the black soot out of my nose. My ribs would actually be sore from bouncing around all day in a car not meant to drive down old farm roads. These were long days filled with uncertainty, anxiety, and downright excitement – I was in a foreign country doing something none of my friends could imagine.

Among the uncertain, anxiety-inducing things to do in Colombia when you don't speak Spanish is finding clean water and something to eat. I learned to say, "*Por favor yo quiero comida...*" which, in broken Spanish means "Please, I would like food." I was in a small village outside of Bogota one day and asked to stop for food. The guy asked in Spanish if "this was okay" and pointed to a little store in the town square of the village. Not knowing what other options there were I said, "*Sí, Sí, Sí. Es* OK. *Gracias.*" It was a little shop that sold coffee and small pastries along with cigarettes and gum. I was afraid to drink water as this was before bottled water was so big. The only meat-like substance was a ham croquette, everything else was sweet pastries, so I ordered a coffee and ham croquette.

My days as a truck driver made me a hardcore black coffee drinker who despises milk and sugar additives. Colombians love a drink known as *Café Con Leche*, which I now know translates to "coffee with milk." *Yuck*. What else was I going to do? I gulped down my ham sort-of sandwich and sipped this horrible coffee with what I assumed was a layer of milk skim across the top. As I was trying to figure out how I was going to drink this, I saw a cow on a nose ring tied to a post in the ditch on the side of the road. If you've never seen a ditch in a third world country, it is full of muddy water and trash. I sat there thinking, this cow must be eating trash, drinking polluted water, and I bet this is where the milk came from in my coffee. I took a sip. The skim layer stuck to my lip and I burned the heck out of my lower lip and chin. "Man that was hot, I hate this *Café Con Leche*," I said. I never drank it again.

Later, I learned of ways to get water that was safe to drink. I had to ask for *Agua con gas*, which translates to "water with bubbles." It is always processed, filtered, clean water that's safe to drink in a sealed bottle. They say Perrier water is an acquired taste, and it was one I acquired by having no choice but to drink bubbled water in Colombia. It wasn't a Perrier, but it was close enough.

On my third or fourth visit to Colombia, I found myself really sick – likely from something I ate. I thought I would die during the long flight back. Sweat was dripping down my entire body as I experienced fever and chills. All I could think of was, *they are not going to let me back in the United States, I'll likely be thrown in quarantine for who knows how long.* Since that trip, I learned bottled water was the way to go even when brushing your teeth. As a result of earthquakes and poor construction, most of my hotel and apartment stays in those times offered brown water flowing for a few seconds whenever you turned on a faucet or shower. It was just the way it was back then.

Colombia was and is an interesting place with challenges at every step. Looking for safe food and safe travel against the backdrop of a 40-year civil war made it an exciting place to work and travel, at least to me.

CHAPTER FOUR: UNINTENTIONAL DRUG WAR VIOLENCE EXPERIENCES

After five or so years I moved fairly freely throughout Colombia. Pablo Escobar was dead and there was still a raging civil war, but at least buildings were not  bombed daily – weekly *maybe* but not daily. Kidnapping was mainly a domestic or big corporation issue. No one wanted a little player like me, at least that's what I believed. But still, the civil unrest and narco-trafficking continued to torment this beautiful country. While many might still drive by fields of robust marijuana plants occasionally, cocaine was the number one cash crop of Colombia and was hidden mostly in the jungles – not on the side of the road.

I was visiting some farms during one trip, riding with a grower friend of mine. After a full day of farm visits, my friend suggested we stop at a carnation farm on the way back to town. It would be our one last stop. "Oh, let's just pull in here and take a quick look," he said, telling me about the farm as well as the day before when the guerrillas had been there. They shot the farm's guards and locked the staff in the flower coolers. I said that I didn't need to see this farm since I had already seen so many farms that day, but despite my pleas we did a quick tour. Nothing happened, but it became clear to me how abnormality had become normal in Colombia. FARC fighters were often sent to move throughout a region on foot, as they were not a formal military with troop transport. As they walked the countryside they would often stop at farms or small businesses and take what they wanted – food, clothing, rest, or money. They typically took whatever they wanted by force and killed whoever resisted. Even today, the fighters still rule entire villages in the more remote parts of the country. Recently, I read an article which described FARC rebels killing people for not wearing a mask in light of the COVID-19 pandemic – scary and disturbing.

Owners of farms in the 1990s often traveled in armored cars and used radios to check on guerrilla activity before venturing out of the city. Despite the violence and armored cars, after a year and multiple trips to Columbia, I rented a small packing room corner on a flower farm in a town named Suba. With this move I became an exporter and importer of flowers into the U.S.

I used the farm for specialty packing and to assemble flower bunches together for our supermarket customers. The grower allowed me to rent both the space and labor during his workers' time off. We used both flowers from his farm and those I procured from other growers to create bouquets and consumer bunches. I traveled to Colombia with a hard suitcase full of plastic flower sleeves, big flower cutters, and a considerable amount of cash. The cash was used to pay workers, drivers, and anyone else who needed cash to get something done in the developing nation. In hindsight traveling with cash was not a smart thing to do, but, I learned quickly there wasn't much I couldn't resolve with a fist full of dollars in Colombia.

My bouquet operation was coming along quite nicely, but it didn't make me immune to Colombian guerrilla violence. I used to stay at the Bogota Plaza as it was the closest thing to an American hotel. It offered a bilingual staff, so I didn't have to embarrass myself with my terrible Spanglish. The hotel's location also made it easier to hire inconspicuous drivers who would take me to various meetings. As much as I enjoyed my stays in the hotel, a bomb exploded on one of the floors two weeks after one of my visits. The explosion took out most of the floor, and I unsurprisingly lost interest in staying there. Sure, no one was looking to blow me up since I was an insignificant, low-key importer, but that didn't mean guerrillas didn't want to bomb the people staying in the rooms next to me. I never knew who might be staying in the room next to me or what other people might want to do to them.

I stayed a few times in the Hotel Tequendama since it had a great casino where I felt like a big man playing blackjack with my stacks of pesos. The Tequendama was bombed in the 80s and some 20 years later, I saw a documentary on Escobar and learned his wife and children were holed up for several months at the Tequendama under military protection while the Cali Drug Cartel sought to kill them or lure Pablo out of hiding trying to rescue them. I'm not sure if any of my stays overlapped their "stay," but again, I never knew who was in the room next to me and if someone wanted them dead.

I decided to banish such concerns from my mind. A grower I had gotten to know pretty well offered to set me up in the *Andinos Apartmentes*. The apartments were in a small, quiet neighborhood "off the grid" as I liked to call it and I stayed there for one to two week intervals throughout the year. The street was sectioned off with an armed military at two gates on either end of the road just off Calle 100, a major avenue downtown. Cab drivers who took me to *Andinos* had their cars inspected for bombs, including under the vehicles and inside the trunks. I didn't mind this at all because it helped me feel safe. Or did it? I also saw in that same documentary that the reason they searched trucks was because they were looking for Escobar who while he was on the run had been traveling in the trunk of a taxi driven by one of his *sicarios* (assassins). I had no idea at the time as this seemed a commonplace occurrence.

My sense of security wouldn't last, however. In those days, going to South America always meant staying for a week or two because traveling there wasn't nearly as easy as it had been in the prior 15 years. One day I was in my apartment, working at my desk, and listening to the birds chirping sweetly outside my window. The fresh mountain air was flowing through my room and adding to my sensory experience when suddenly I heard automatic gunfire in the street below.

I rushed to the window to see people scrambling frantically as more gunfire rang out. I couldn't see where it was coming from, but I knew it had to be close. Then it hit me – well, the gunfire didn't hit me, but I realized hanging out the window like a dummy made it easy to get caught in the crossfire. Not wanting to die senselessly, I ducked down and sat on the floor, my heart beating rapidly. I began working out in my head where the safest place in the room was in the likelihood of a stray bullet making its way inside. I asked myself what I was going to do if they stormed my building and determined where my exit points were. Colombia will teach you situational awareness at all times, something that took only a short time to learn. The shooting ceased after a few minutes, but I was reminded again that I was far from home and had to have significantly different considerations in mind if I was going to keep traveling to Colombia without getting kidnapped or shot.

I was telling a friend of mine this story as he picked me up one night for dinner. He said, "You know I always wondered why you stay here, this is a Colombian Mafia neighborhood and the former mayor of the city also lives here." After some thought he figured it was probably safe because the mafia was here, but it could be dangerous if someone came after the ex-mayor. The former mayor was very politically powerful, and Colombia has a bloody history of killing powerful political figures. It was and is part of the complexity of Colombia where criminals and politicians live on the same street and enjoy military protection. If you ever watch a documentary on the Colombian prison system, the inmates have guns and the prison system relies on them to police themselves via these prison gangs with guns – strange place indeed.

One morning as I was contemplating my safety and waiting in the apartment lobby for a car to pick me up, I noticed another American. It wasn't commonplace to see Americans in those apartments, so my interest was piqued. We exchanged pleasantries and he began to question why I was in Colombia. He showed much interest in hearing about the country's floral industry, and I was happy to talk about it.

After a few minutes he told me he was with the DEA (Drug Enforcement Administration) and asked if I would consider working with the organization or becoming an agent. Colombia was obviously a drug hot spot and the administration needed people who knew their way around. I began imagining myself running around the country in a *Miami Vice*-style suit with rolled-up sleeves and shoes without socks, thinking I was ready to do it.

Time passed and I didn't call him, though I did look into how one joined the DEA and what the requirements were. One of them was a college education, something I didn't have and about which I was very self-conscious. Someone in my family once wrote in a letter to my wife that I will never forget saying, "I do worry about Robert's lack of formal education, it is often the deciding factor in business and he will never be the social equal of those with a good education."

I worked hard throughout my 30s and 40s trying not to let those comments define me.

Down the street from my apartment in Bogota was a Japanese steakhouse, and one night several cars pulled up to the establishment when a group of men entered. The growers with whom I was dining became visibly agitated, and quickly put down enough cash to cover our food and drinks. They rushed me into their car and down the road, telling me the men were "narco" traffickers and the steakhouse was no longer somewhere I wanted to be. The Cali and Medellin drug cartels, once united as the world's largest cocaine producers, were now at war with each other. No one on either side was safe anywhere in Colombia and everyone in their proximity was at risk of being caught in the crossfire. Gunfights between the cartels plagued the cities during those times. It seemed it was time to reassess my business goals and consider moving to a safer country.

In the past 15 years or so, with Pablo Escobar gone and the advent of state-of-the-art technology, travel to Colombia is much easier, with effective communication and quality accommodations with major brands like Hilton and Hyatt.

CHAPTER FIVE: My Beginning is a Look Back

I was born in September of 1969 in Reynolds Army Hospital, Fort Sill, Oklahoma. My mother used to joke that she knew I would be a handful because it took two special forces soldiers to help bring me into the world. They happened to be there because of medical residency training and my mother was certainly grateful for their assistance.

As a military family, moving constantly was normal. I was fortunate to spend time overseas as a child, including Germany where my father was attached to a NATO unit playing cat and mouse with the Soviets using nuclear missiles during the cold war. Our time as a family in Europe came immediately after my father's service in Vietnam.

As a kid growing up on the move I bounced between being a good kid and a not-so-good kid depending on the year and who I came into contact with at each new school. After going through my mother's belongings following her passing, I found she had saved every school report card. When I put them into chronological order, I realized growing up as an Army brat and bouncing between divorced parents, I had never spent two full years at any one school. The longest was a year and a half, which I believe helped to explain my sometimes-erratic childhood.

In 1984, I was sent to Florida for a summer vacation with my mother. My father had been transferred to the 2nd Infantry Division, South Korea. Little did I know at the time that I wasn't on vacation but would never return to my friends at Ft. Lee in Virginia, where I had been living. Growing up, I just went where my parents told me, and while I never got used to it, I really didn't know any different. Every move was a good move in my opinion. I learned to adapt to quick moving changes and each move offered an opportunity for reinvention.

When I moved in with my mom and her new husband in Florida, so began my adventures in the floral industry. My stepfather owned a farm in Central Florida where he grew potted plants, and he gave me a job when I was 14. My father provided my moral and ethical military-based foundation of right or wrong," and my stepfather provided a business opportunity and foundation for a career. Some complain about their divorce-themed childhoods, of bouncing around among parents, schools, and friends, yet I feel everything I experienced along the way made me a better, more understanding person, so no complaints here.

I met one of my first bosses/mentors in life while hard at work on the family farm. His name was Benny Turner and he probably felt like my babysitter at times, but he was kind enough to never show it. Benny's skin was so eaten up by chemicals it looked like it might fall from his face, and sadly he passed away at a relatively young age from severe exposure to agro-chemicals. He taught me how to weed, feed, pull, and pack plants. When we sprayed chemicals, we often took our shirts and shoes off to keep them from getting soaked in what we were spraying, a practice which rarely happens now as proper coveralls are an industry safety *must*.

Benny was an old school kind of guy who believed in the power of hard work. His life was the greenhouse, and because of him I received my first lesson in environmentally friendly control practices on farms. He would instruct me to mix rock salt in a bucket of water, then pour the mixture over weeds outside the greenhouse to retard their growth. Salt was less expensive and a more natural way of killing weeds. Benny also had me create a soapy water mixture to spray on the plants surrounding the greenhouse to kill aphids and mealybugs who turn our greenery to brown.

While outside the greenhouse was all about destroying weeds and pests using the least harmful methods, inside was all business, all the time. The worst agro-chemicals were used on a regimented application schedule and often featured heavy mixes. I have fond memories of the farm for many reasons, including the fact that Benny championed eco-friendly techniques before "eco-friendly" was even a term. Benny was probably the greatest example of why someone should desire a different career due to the physical toll it took, but a job as a grower was all I wanted at the time.

CHAPTER SIX : Dumb Decisions Somehow

Equaled Promotions

It's funny for me to think about it now, but many of the career promotions I've enjoyed stemmed from something stupid I did. If I remember correctly, the first promotion happened when I was loading a stack of empty, flat boxes on the seat rest of a golf cart at the greenhouse. Those boxes quickly slid from the seat and landed on the gas pedal, sending the driver-free cart careening down an aisle between two plant beds and through the side of the greenhouse. I was subsequently "promoted" to lawn mowing where I could inflict less damage.

Lawn mowing was enjoyable since the mower was the rider variety. Benny had me mow twice in alternate directions to maintain a "turf level." By doing so, I provided the lawn with clean, precise cuts that benefited grass root systems and didn't cause detrimental tears of the leaves. It was a technique similar to pruning, which prompted me to view Benny in a Mr. Myogi, "wax on, wax off" way. I didn't think much of the practice at the time, but now I realize I was developing a strong work ethic and taking pride in jobs done well.

In addition to perfecting my grass cutting techniques, I started riding with the farm's delivery drivers to set up Winn Dixie stores, our largest customer at the time. Since I was 15 they would drop me off at a store that needed to be cleaned up and re-merchandised, then pick me up after their deliveries for a ride back to the warehouse. When I turned 16, I began driving the trucks and vans myself. I ditched school frequently as a result but racked up *serious* work hours. Over the next few years I held the company record for most hours worked in a week and in a single day. One day I worked 34 hours straight and somehow managed not to collapse. I had set up a Winn Dixie store for a grand opening. Back then we installed artificial plants and flowers over the cash registers in all new stores as part of the décor. There was a particular set which caused someone in middle management to say, "No artificials in this store, they're too expensive."

The morning of the grand opening, I arrived at 4 a.m. as usual to put last-minute touches on the floral department before the store opened. An hour before the opening, the division president for Winn Dixie came in, wrapped his arm around me, and walked me up to the registers asking, "Do you notice something missing up here, son?" he said, adding "I want this install done before this store opens tomorrow morning."

"Yes sir, I'll handle it," I replied. I called back to the warehouse to have all the materials and supplies delivered to the store by the end of the day. I finished out my scheduled day then all night after the store closed, staying on the ladder arranging silk flowers.

By 4 a.m. all of my produce department buddies rolled in and said, "Wow, you're *still here*?" They were probably amazed not to find me in a crumpled heap next to the ladder.

Around 2 p.m. I left the store and headed home to crash. Home was over an hour away, but I made it! I had worked 34 hours straight. A long day, right? Another time I worked 110 hours in a week. I would come in at 4 a.m. to drive, then work with the production team—sometimes until 2 a.m. – day after day for seven days straight. These were typical hours for a holiday like Valentine's, but I made sure I got in earlier and stayed later. Aside from just wanting to win, I got time and half pay, so I couldn't understand why everyone didn't work insane hours. Back in the day I made $3.75/hour, so at time and a half I was clocking away at $5.60/hour which was as much as some grown men made working 40 hours a week! I was making *two* full time checks. During this period of my career I would typically wake up at 4 a.m. for my normal route, then get back in the afternoon to have the boss say, "Go get a rental truck, I need you to deliver to Nashville by tomorrow." I loved the challenge and made many late night/early morning runs, both local and out of state.

Even as a kid, those late night/early morning runs eventually made me tired. I remember one early morning around 2 a.m. I was driving down the interstate for hours, and my eyes were getting droop, droop, droopy. It was then that I learned a valuable lesson about Vivran or "No Doze Caffeine" pills, which were the 1980s equivalent to RedBull. I bought some caffeine pills at a truck stop and took one, then another, *and another* to try and stay awake. It wasn't working—*well, so I thought*---and I was still tired.

I took a few more and quickly learned it was *not* a magic pill to pep you up. But – when mixed with pure, natural adrenaline, the stuff sends you on a trip to the moon. Past the moon, actually. I was driving down I-75 at 2 a.m. with a slower car in front of me, so I moved to the passing lane. Just as I got ready to pass, the car sped up. I ducked back behind him in the right lane for a mile or so, then he slowed down again. I moved left to pass and he did the same thing. We did this for several miles, irritating me more and more as we went. Many trucks have what's known as a "governor" to keep them from going more than a certain miles per hour, so I couldn't just blow past him but I had had enough. Having recently watched the movie *Top Gun,* I said to myself, "I'll slam on the brakes and he'll fly right by, get way up in front of me, and I won't have to deal with this."

It was then that the caffeine pills kicked in. I got really mad and slammed on the brakes *way* harder than I wanted to, hitting them hard as the adrenaline took over my system. The truck wheels locked up, the dashboard lights illuminated, alarms blared, air brake sensors went off, and the truck started violently bucking up and down. I looked over my front right quarter panel with the truck bucking like crazy, and went back and forth between seeing the car and not seeing it, thinking, *My God, I've run over and killed these poor people!*

All of it happened pretty darned fast and I got the truck under control, glancing in the rear view mirrors and back to where the car had stayed very clear of me. I never saw him again. I can't imagine the fear in his eyes watching this out-of-control vehicle almost ride over him like a monster truck over a Mazda. When I hear of late night, over-the-road truck accidents, I know exactly how these things can happen. I was very lucky that night and so was the car driver.

As much as I enjoyed my newfound status as a driver, putting a young kid behind the wheel so often was probably not the best idea. One day I was driving a box van down Highway 50 in Central Florida heading to the city of Titusville, not realizing a ticket was in my immediate future. My competitive nature made me want to be first no matter what and beat the older drivers in deliveries. I also wanted to be the first one back to the warehouse, the first to get second runs, the first everything. While barreling down the interstate in route to Titusville, a local sheriff's deputy got in front of me – he was driving 50 miles per hour in a 55 mph zone.

Being the dumb kid I was, I decided to ride his bumper for about two miles, then make my move to pass him. Once I cleared his car I made the genius decision to flick a cigarette butt out the window. I didn't give the act a second thought since it was commonplace back then – everyone flicked their butts out the window. The officer's vehicle lights immediately illuminated and he pulled me over. The policeman started yelling at me, asking me how dumb I could really be. My cigarette butt had apparently hit his windshield and he was shouting, "I could write you a ticket for following too closely to a law enforcement vehicle, exceeding the speed limit, illegally changing lanes, and intentionally creating a fire hazard!"

I apologized profusely, saying many "Yes, sirs" and "No, sirs" along the way. Being from a military family, I was respectful despite suffering from teenage dumbness. The cop graciously sent me on my way, ticket-free, but the next day I got pulled over again for speeding. I was driving on Highway 50 again on the opposite side of the state, this time heading to Brooksville. The officer gave me a written warning and told me to slow down.

After receiving my written warning, I got pulled over *again*. I was just a few miles down the road and scrambling like a maniac to shove the written warning under my seat. I only got a verbal warning from the officer, but I was clearly getting out of control. Yes, a chauffeur license could get you behind the wheel back then because commercial driver's licenses (CDL) weren't a thing, but that didn't excuse my reckless "Speed Racer" ways.

In those days I was a dangerous but very proficient driver. We had box trucks with open cabs and I was always proud of my ability to fix my box loads while speeding down the road at 55 miles per hour. I could set the truck straight, quickly run to the back, pick up a fallen stack of boxes, and get back to my seat before the truck veered into the lane next to me. Later, I carried an axe handle in my truck so I could wedge it in between the seat and gas pedal to keep the truck going down the road. Now I call it "country boy cruise control."

A few months later the company's insurance company kicked me off the policy since I was too much of a liability. Since I was a diligent worker, not to mention family, I was brought into the office to be a buyer. My stupid decisions got me promoted once more. First, I worked in hardgoods, then plants, and finally flowers. I worked just as hard at buying as I did at delivering and lawn mowing, enjoying processes such as introducing new suppliers to our company and negotiating prices to improve our sales prices and gross margins. I loved the challenge of making deals. My mind was a sponge and I loved learning who produced what and how I could get closer to the source in every instance.

CHAPTER SEVEN: Wise Guys and One Nasty Hurricane

As I brought in new sources of hardgoods and new growers of plants from around the country, I naturally started selling to our largest customer. I had worked with these people doing store sets and grand openings so as they got promoted, I got promoted to leverage my relationships. I did a pretty good job, especially brokering plants to Winn Dixie from growers nationwide. Brokering was a good business where you made 20 percent for selling plants to supermarkets and placing delivery orders from farms. All I did was invoice and if there was a quality problem, the supermarket refused the load and the loss was on the grower. It was the first time I was threatened in the industry but it was not the last.

I was dealing with a company in New York that seemed to have control over some greenhouses in their state as well as New Jersey and North Carolina, of all places. I met the men behind the greenhouses through a friend and they acted like real wise guys. They were always giving out boxes of cigars or cookies made in Little Italy, NY. You would think these were "made" guys.

The mafia involved in flowers? It didn't seem likely, but I loved *The Godfather and Goodfellas,* so I found it fun to hang out with them at trade shows and on the casino boats we used to take out of Ft. Lauderdale after hours. I did business with them for around nine months before we ran into our first rejected load of plants for Winn Dixie. So as normal, I let the farm know the load was kicked and they needed to either take the plants back to New York or sell them elsewhere. I immediately got a call from the company. The guy on the phone said, "The 'boss' wants to talk to you."

This guy was right out of a movie. I'd never met him before, but he was very aggressive and told me I needed to resolve my problem because his truck "wasn't going anywhere until it was unloaded." Being in my early 20s and five-plus years into my career I was fairly confident in myself, saying "Buddy, I'm not sure who you think you're talking to, but your truckload of garbage better get down the road before I bill you for storage by the day."

He replied, "My friend, do you know what we do with people like you? What size shoe are you? I'm guessing a 10 or 11, and I'm going to fit you some new flippers for your next swim." Obviously referencing the cliche gangster movie of pouring concrete on your feet to weigh you down and dropping you off a bridge into deep water, never to be found again. Jimmy Hoffa is still MIA, you know.

I had just come back from my first trip to Bogota and was watching *way* too many episodes of *Miami Vice,* so I replied, "My friend, do you know what a Colombian Necktie is?"

There was a moment of awkward silence and I wondered if he didn't get the reference. Then he laughed and said, "I like you Robert, let's do a better job next time of finding an alternate place to sell if a load gets kicked again."

I'm still not sure if he was kidding, but later his son told me at a trade show that his dad "really liked me" and he doesn't like many people. The son also said he had never seen his dad take a loss on a load like that before which left me feeling quite proud.

Many of the new farms I was buying from were in Homestead, Florida, just south of Miami on the edge of the gator-infested Everglades. I had some pretty good friends I worked with there, in particular at one farm owned by a Dutch company. I was at the farm one late summer day looking over upcoming holiday crops and found the owner in Holland was expanding the operation, much like many others in those days. The owner sent three guys from Holland to come and install the new greenhouses. These guys had never been to the U.S., and were young and full of energy.

Dutch people work hard and when work is done, they can play hard. These guys were told to fly into Ft. Lauderdale, rent a car, and drive to the greenhouse. Once they cleared immigration, they rented a Ferrari and drove to Homestead knowing their boss was going to kill them when he saw the bill. By the time I had gotten there, they had been working for weeks and had nearly all the greenhouses up. These guys worked hard but were ready to party since they were youngsters. The sales guy for the farm and I decided to take them out on the town and let them burn off some steam. We did our best to show them a good time, taking them to a few less-than-desirable places. Those Dutchmen could put back a large volume of beer...and honestly it's about all I can remember about that night. I arrived at the farm the next day around 8 a.m. and they were back hard at work on the greenhouses like it never happened.

Just three weeks later in 1992, Hurricane Andrew blazed a path through South Florida. The eye passed right over Homestead and it was one of the worst hurricanes in U.S. history. After seeing the next-day images on the news, I knew we had to do something. There was no word from the Dutchmen, so we had no idea if they survived. Their plan had been to stay on the farm and sleep in the office in case they needed to protect the greenhouses they had just built.

Back in Orlando, we spent two days gathering aid – water, food, clothing, and even vet-donated dog food in case we ran across the pets – to take to Homestead. The plan was I would drive a truckload of supplies in and see if we could find them. Not knowing what to expect, I hit the road early in the morning.

Homestead was a beautiful, tropical area of Florida. Papaya and mango trees grew together over the streets, often making it like driving through a tunnel. As I approached Homestead in the truck it quickly became clear this was no longer the same place. I started seeing trucks turned over on their side, dead cattle along the road, and telephone poles snapped in half. National Guard troops were directing traffic to passable roads and helicopters were overhead, landing in fields to drop off more troops. Street signs were gone so I had to navigate by feel where the troops would allow me to go versus where I thought the farm was located. Nothing looked the same. As I passed a few farms I knew had existed just a few weeks ago, I only saw empty fields of white sand. Everything was wiped away and I wondered, *Where did it all go? Naples? Out in the Gulf of Mexico?* Entire greenhouse structures were gone.

I finally arrived at the farm's greenhouse to find the Dutchmen working again, sifting through the mess that was left. Every greenhouse, new and old, was blown down to the ground. These were big steel greenhouses that weren't supposed to blow away, but blew down they did. Hearing the stories of the Dutchmen and how their first visit to the U.S. included the eye of a hurricane was inspiring. These guys were naturally terrified, especially when the roof of the office in which they had stayed was torn off but the four concrete walls remained. They said the storm sounded like a train bearing down, making them think they would become part of the greenhouse rubble. What a visit to the U.S. – holed up in a small, four-wall concrete farm building under the desks with more than half the roof gone.

We unloaded my truck with supplies for anyone at the farm and surrounding farms. Migrant workers came out from nearby properties and we shared everything we had. These people picked through the mounds of clothes we brought, a pallet of water, and even the dogs got food from our offerings. For our friends at the greenhouse, we brought a gas grill and cooler full of hot dogs and hamburgers, and cooked everything we had until everyone got enough to eat. It was going to be a long rebuilding for all these people, and we gave a day or two of our help with what we had brought. I'd never seen anything like it – farms that I had done business with for years were completely gone.

By this time I was the president of multiple companies. We had a growing operation in Apopka, a supermarket production company, a brokerage for plants, an event decor company with contracts at some of the top resorts in Central Florida, and the bouquet division in Colombia.

CHAPTER EIGHT: Moving to Ecuador

Heading back to the cut flower side of the business – after a few years running the bouquet company in Colombia and assessing the risk versus rewards – I saw an opportunity in Ecuador just over the border. Many of my Colombian friends had moved to Miami to flee the civil and drug wars still raging in Colombia.

In 1994, I went on a study tour of Ecuador to see what I could learn and who I could meet in the flower business. Ecuador had exploded onto the flower scene in the 1990s, growing the best and most unique rose varieties due to the high altitudes of the farms outside of Quito, its capital. The country is on the equator, meaning it receives a solid 12 hours of light every day, year-round. The equator position also means the sun's rays come straight down instead of on an angle like they do in North America, the rose cultivation conditions are among the world's best. Many people think it's cheap labor that keeps the rose industry alive in Ecuador, but it's actually the outstanding growing conditions. China has some of the cheapest labor in the world but lacks equatorial growing locations at more than 9,500 feet above sea level.

During my time in Ecuador, the country started producing the latest varieties of roses which people worldwide were scrambling to purchase. The roses had big heads and long stems, and soon "everyone and their cousins" were operating rose farms. These farms were so profitable one could plant the blooms and have bank loans paid down after the first Valentine's Day order bonanza. It's a more challenging market now, but in the '90s it was the gold rush of the floral industry. I moved my operation to Ecuador because I witnessed this phenomenon, thinking I would be one of the first Americans on the scene with such a business. Easy peasy, right? Well, not exactly.

I started and ran the company much like its Colombia counterpart. I made deals with growers to use their facilities and lease their labor to create our products. I also met a rose grower, who became the first person in Ecuador from whom I purchased. A wealthy man, he made his fortune as an arms dealer for the Ecuadorian military. He was also a consultant for a U.S. oil company in Ecuador, these jobs which made him very successful. I had plenty of respect for this very influential person but always wondered just how connected he was since he frequently dined with the President of Ecuador and lived with no fear due to relationships with the military. Ecuador was at war with Peru in 1981 and again in 1995 so the military spent a lot of money with this gentleman and I wondered why he was running a rose farm. We became friends and remained so until his passing in the early 2000s. I was consulting for his farm prior to his passing when his children took over and in just a few short years that part of his legacy was gone.

The one thing I did differently in the Ecuador operation was to form the equivalent of a corporation to run the business. We would not be just packaging for our own use, we would start selling to other importers the packaged products for their customers. Being twenty-something, I had never started a corporation, and certainly not in a foreign country, so this was a true learning experience. I hired an attorney in Quito and off we rode into the corporate sunset, covered as it was with red tape.

It took me four or five months and many trips to Ecuador to set up the corporation, sign documents, and meet with legal and accounting people to do it correctly. Accounting was going to be interesting in light of two currencies and two sets of tax laws. My education in General Accounting 101 was now on an international level with much trust in some pretty shady places. I spent a considerable amount of time winding through a maze of legal and tax consequences, with advice often contradicting itself or manifesting without regard for laws in one country or the other. But sometimes you just have to go for it. The difference between those who *do* and those who *never do* is having the guts actually do it and learn along the way. At least that was my thinking, and I'm probably pretty lucky nothing bad happened to me on my new accounting front and many others.

The biggest hurdle with accounting practices in Ecuador was everyone kept two sets of books. I didn't particularly care for this concept and wanted to run my operation like I did our business in the U.S. My newly hired accountant in Ecuador kept saying, "No, you can't do that," so we had many philosophical and legal debates on how to manage the business.

During this period in Ecuador I paid tax based on the value of the product I was exporting – just like everyone else. So, if I sold roses to a customer in the U.S. for $0.65 a stem, growers to minimize their taxes would report $0.25 a stem on a commercial export invoice, then $0.65 on an actual invoice. Tax was paid based on $0.25. I wanted to declare the *actual* $0.65 and have one set of books. It just seemed easier and more likely to keep me out of an Ecuadorian prison for tax evasion. Simple, right? I figured I would forcefully tell the accountant, "This is what I'm doing."

Well, he gave me a very direct and bone-chilling reason not to manage the business my way. "The problem here is that every other farm declares $0.25 and you're wanting to go out at $0.65," he told me, tut-tutting my one-book-to-rule-them-all idea. "That's going to cause the government to look at the other farms and say, 'Gee, why aren't you declaring $0.65???'"

"Um, that's not really my problem, is it?" I replied, steadfast in my resolve to take the ethical and legal high ground.

"Well, unfortunately you will create a lot of enemies in Ecuador, and while we are a peaceful nation, sometimes people handle those they don't like a little differently than you might see in the U.S…this makes sense, no????" the accountant queried with an unblinking, unsettling stare.

"*Sí* Señor, *es muy claro* – I see your point," I replied.

Again, I was reminded that I was not in Kansas anymore, or anywhere within that particular Tristate Area.
I needed a quick solution to this problem and an accountant in the U.S. who understood international and national tax laws. I reached out and made an appointment with the best one I could find. Back in the day there was what was known as the "Big 10" accounting firms, but in today's world following mergers and acquisitions I think it's now the "Big Three."

I went to these big dogs who had a penthouse office in the financial district in Miami overlooking Key Biscayne. Two gentlemen took me to the conference room and we had an overview discussion on my business in Ecuador and the U.S., then dove into exactly why I was there. I explained my meetings with the Ecuadorian accountant and how I needed help solving my two-book system conundrum.

"Listen Robert," one of them said, gently mopping his brow, "We do this for a lot of companies. It's really easy, we will set up a corporate trust for you in the Cayman Islands and you funnel only the money you need for your Ecuador operation back to Ecuador. Use your Cayman company to sell flowers to your U.S. customers in dollars with a 30 percent markup," he continued. "Buy the flowers from your Ecuadorian company and ship them directly to the U.S. When your customer pays you in your Cayman account, you can send what you need to pay your Ecuadorian grower and workers. Simply convert the dollars to *sucres* (Ecuador's monetary unit) and leave the rest of the money safe in Cayman."

"Wow," I thought. "This seems like a great idea!" It was still a two-book system, but not two books in Ecuador. But again, having watched endless *Miami Vice* episodes, I was a little suspicious of banking in the Caymans since drug dealers banked there, and banked there often.

"So what do I do with this money in the Caymans?" I inquired.

"Do whatever you want with it," he replied. "It will be in a trust and no one will know what's there. Not the U.S. government, not creditors, not even an ex-wife. No one."

I asked if it was, you know, *legal* to have money in a hidden account like that since I was too young to be looking over my shoulders for the next 50 years.

"As a U.S. tax citizen, you are required to report any income you earn anywhere in the world on your U.S. tax return," he explained in a canned legal reply.

Back then, the first $75K I made would be exempt from U.S. taxes, but I still had to report it. I thought, *Well, that contradicts what he just said about putting it in trust and no one will ever know, not even the IRS.* So I quizzed him again. The second man left at this juncture, making it a conversation with only two people to hear. We went back and forth a few times on what they can do for me versus what is legal, and I was shocked at the *downright unlawful* advice I was getting on international money movements from a "Big 10" accounting firm. I was learning a lot about business, leaving my old textbooks in the dust, and moving right into Reality 101.

Ultimately I never hired the firm, but I did go to Cayman to open a company, sell my products, and keep excess money *out* of Ecuadorian banks. At the time every dollar I brought into Ecuador had to be converted to the *sucre* through the national central bank. You could convert back to dollars, but for every $1 in – only $0.75 came out due to exchange rates and fees.

Little did I know but keeping excess money out of Ecuador would save me big in the future. In the late 90s, Ecuador went through a massive currency crisis. On my first trip to the South American country, it had an exchange rate of 800 *sucres* to the dollar, then it spiked and eventually got pegged by the government at 25,000 *sucres* per dollar. The problem was so bad that one day the Ecuadorian government froze everyone's accounts, and for six months you could only withdraw a small amount each week. The government was earning interest on everyone's money to regain liquidity in its own currency. Thank God I had cash safely tucked away in the Cayman Islands. I got some good advice from that Miami accounting firm, unscrupulous as they were.

CHAPTER NINE: Business Expansions, Ethical Crises, and Corrupt Politicians

After a year or two of spending a week of every month in Ecuador, it was time to expand. It was also time for the business to become less reliant on me, the perpetual fish out of water.

I met and rented space from a man I call a friend now some 25 years later. He was an American with Ecuadorian heritage and had come to Ecuador in the early 80s to work with his family's land. The guy was full of adventure stories which had transpired 5 years before my visit, so clearly I was not the first gringo on the moon.

He owned a medium size flower farm in Ecuador, and I was renting space and labor from him before we decided to partner in this venture. With his experience, the facilities he owned in Ecuador, and my experience selling to supermarkets in the U.S., we would be the largest exporter of bouquets and supermarket bunches.

I was always convinced everything I did was going to make me the best in the world. Nothing was unachievable in my mind. My new friend in Ecuador went to a fancy boarding school outside of Washington D.C., where his father or grandfather was an Ecuadorian Ambassador to the United States, so he had some pretty interesting connections at the capital. We hired a "kid" he knew who had attended the same school and had recently graduated from a prestigious college with a degree in English. It seemed like a logical choice for this "kid" to come to Ecuador and manage a flower company. He was bilingual and after a few weeks in Ecuador his Spanish was good enough to manage our production crew and purchasing needs. We bought him a pickup truck to get around, and I finally had my own gringo driver.

Not only did he adopt the language, he quickly fell into the culture in Ecuador. After a few short months, I noticed he was *always* late to pick me up and for meetings. It raised my eyebrows, though it shouldn't have, because two things are common knowledge in Ecuador, at least as stereotypes go – Ecuadorians are always late and they have no sense of humor about themselves. Even today I can schedule back-to-back meetings at my hotel in Ecuador every hour on the hour and by the second meeting we will be behind schedule. I grew up in a military family where if you were not 10 minutes early, you were 15 minutes late – no exceptions. In Ecuador *everyone* is 15 to 30 minutes late and will walk in and say, "Wow, traffic was terrible, you cannot believe how bad it was."

To me, if you know traffic is bad every day, you leave 30 minutes early and you're never late. Anyway, my new manager was late for literally every meeting.

One day we were outside of the city visiting farms when we got pulled over for speeding. I'd never seen anyone pulled over for speeding in Ecuador, but had heard it was a shakedown scam concerning local cops craving money. My new manager was driving, asking me over and over what he should do.

"Well, ask him what the cost is if we pay here," I said, trying to take the non-bribe way to eliminate the problem.

My suggestion made the cop really mad, apparently the stereotype of cops shaking down gringos for money is either a huge myth or something that happens only in other countries. He was *livid*. We took our ticket and went about our way shaking with anxiety over that failed transaction.

After a few years of hotel stays in Ecuador and before national chains like Marriott existed, I rented an apartment in Quito. A two-bedroom unit right on the park in central Quito. It featured a bed made of straw and cost $8 a week in housekeeping. Hardly glamorous, but it sufficed. Where else in my world could I get a full housekeeper for $8 a week? If I paid $12 she would do laundry too. I'm not sure where she washed my clothes, but they always came back hard like sandpaper. I always pictured her beating them on a rock down by a stream. It probably was not a nice assumption, and she was a very nice lady who worked very hard for her money. I always tipped her 40 percent of the bill, it just didn't seem right to pay someone $8 to clean up my mess.

We faced several big challenges in Ecuador those first few years. The financial crisis was one, another was the rioting and protesting during the time. There were so many strikes and protests that every other week the city was shut down. Cab drivers and truckers would strike over increases in gas costs, they would do national service shutdowns and burn tires at strategic street corners to stop traffic and services from moving. The airport was blocked so no flowers could get there and one particular uprising came right at Valentine's Day, creating a crisis for the number one exporter of roses in the world.

When we think of Valentine's Day in the U.S., we think of big, expensive roses and how we must have them. All of the farms in Ecuador got together with the government to find solutions for this problem, because growers would lose millions if they couldn't get flowers to the airport and subsequently U.S. flower shops. Our operation was no different. It was so important to keep the flowers moving that as a group of growers, we hired helicopters to pick blooms up from the farm and fly them to the airport. Those 'copters flew over all the protests and riots, transporting roses for export. Later, the association of floral exporters was able to get military tanks and trucks to escort the flowers to the airport in the dark of night. There were no transportation challenges we didn't encounter, no matter how big or small.

At Thanksgiving one year, we were importing flowers from Colombia and bringing them to our operation in Ecuador where we could make mixed bouquets and assorted boxes using the best products from both countries. Ecuador and Colombia fall under a free trade agreement called the Andean Trade Pact, meaning there were no tariffs or duties to move products between the countries. Yet we still had to pass agriculture and customs inspections. So for this holiday we were behind in production, flying in some flowers from Colombia and, wouldn't you know it, the bull fights were going on and the city was basically shut down as bull fights and soccer traditionally kill productivity in Ecuador.

Our flowers were stuck at the airport, waiting on a signature from an agriculture agent before they could showcase their beauty in assorted American shops. I sent our manager down there and said, "I don't care how you get them released, just make it happen."

Our production crew couldn't finish their run until these flowers showed up. My manager got to the airport and gave $5 to the guy who guards the gate (a typical bribe), then another $5 to get an agent to tell him some rather distressing news. It seemed the only person who could sign this document was the Minister of Agriculture. Where was the minister? Oh, just attending a bull fight.

So off we went to the stadium to find this guy. We pleaded for him to sign the document, prompting a "give me $20" response. Apparently, the Minister of Agriculture of an entire nation needed $20 to do his job – just crazy! A $30 expense total plus four hours equaled no more problems. It is that easy or that challenging to do business in Ecuador depending on your view.

As time went on we had a good lil' business that was growing, pun intended. My partners were a huge blessing, providing new management I just couldn't provide from the U.S. Our manager was doing a good job, but what we *didn't* know was that he was working on his own lil' business on the side. The guy was getting in with local growers, forming his own relationships with *my* customers.

One day I got the oh-so-delightful call that our entire production crew had just quit. Just like that. It was an odd occurrence since workers were usually local, so I couldn't imagine what else they could be doing for work?

I called my partner in Ecuador to see what the heck was happening. He called me back the next day to inform me the manager told our workers they were all fired and also that he conveniently had another job for them at another farm. Off they went. This guy had started his own company using *everything* we taught him, and was driving around in *our* truck making deals for himself. So much for trusting a gringo brought down to manage the place for us.

They say people from Washington D.C. are the most corrupt people in the world. It seems this former manager justified his actions as not only okay, but a sign of him being a bold, young go-getter. We went to the farm and spoke with our workers. We told them they were *not* fired, and they all came back to our operation the next day. Several weeks went by and again we started losing staff to the same guy. It was enough for me, so I said goodbye to the Ecuador operation and focused my efforts on my U.S. businesses, which seemed much more exciting than dealing with unscrupulous managers.

Ecuador, while safer, had all the normal challenges just like Colombia and it was still a third world country. In the early 2000's after 2 decades of traveling there I was having dinner at a local restaurant down the street from my office. Walking at night is a total game changer compared to daytime even in Ecuador and I certainly knew better. As we walked block after block the guy I was with noticed we were being tracked. He said look down the next alleyway all the way to the other side. Sure enough, each alley on the other side were the same guys tracking and looking down the alley at us. After they saw us they would run to the next one and wait to see us pass again. As we looked behind there were a few other guys following up behind us. I had gotten lulled into thinking this was Orlando and just another walk but we were about to be ambushed. About 3-4 more blocks ahead we were heading onto a less populated industrial area that I knew and it was clear this is where they would make their move, we would be boxed in. We remained calm, talked through options when all of a sudden a taxi came by. We quickly waved him down and jumped in, this option popped up and happened in a matter of 60 secs. We could see the guys behind make a run for us, it felt good watching them out of the rear window knowing we just got so lucky and that was the last time I ever walked back at night.

Everything is different when living and working in a foreign country. From cultures, to legal, accounting and security. I've learned a lifetime of lessons doing business in South America and now back in Orlando. Today I manage the normal business challenges far easier than I probably would have had I never left and had these experiences. I've learned to work the problems day by day, not to get excited by the unthinkable things you didn't see coming. Dwelling on what is so unthinkable wastes valuable time in coming up with solutions. I've started a bouquet company in a converted horse barn stall, run companies out of abandoned strawberry lean-to structures and grown sunflowers on the sides of mountains on multiple 200-400 square feet spaces at various micro climates with little to no water. Finding spaces to conduct business, people to help and overcoming challenges is what I have learned to do. Give me a customer with an order and I'll figure out how to fill it. I love what I do and thrive on the challenge. Don't ask my wife if you see her what she thinks about that.

CHAPTER TEN: Importing Flowers + Concealed Carry = Getting Stopped By Florida Drug Enforcement Officers

By the mid-90s in the U.S., I was selling to local supermarkets and was at the top of my game in my own little world. I was a jack of all trades and master of none, a grower of plants and lawn mower extraordinaire. I improved our hardgoods sales and profits, brokered plants with new suppliers and products, and dove into the cut flower world. My efforts took us from buying in Miami to importing directly from the source, which helped our company as we entered the digital age with cellular telephones in our cars. I was flying high.

Phase Two of my education was coming and I had to fly solo. I had been president of our company for a few years and took it into new supply and marketing areas, but I always had support and financial backing. Now after 13 years of hard, challenging, exciting work, it was time to go do something in the rest of the country. Up until then I was mainly a regional player in a global floral industry game. I had never bought a flower in Oregon, California, or Canada. My supermarket experience was in the southeast, the rest of the country had yet to learn of my brilliance…or youthful arrogance…ha-ha.

There is a book somewhere which says it takes 10,000 hours to be proficient in your trade. There are 2,080 work hours in a year, so at the standard 40-hour work week it takes 4.8 years to be proficient. I've worked 60-70 hours a week most of my life and I was now at 13 years with the same company. So yes, it was *definitely* time for me to fly, much like the REO Speedwagon song.

I left the company, opened a U.S. corporation, and began consulting for a few wholesalers who wanted to buy directly from farms. It was a beautiful time when supermarkets were consolidating their buying powers at the regional division to corporate, going more Miami importer-direct cutting out regional middlemen. For regional players, it was more important than ever to shift their buying habits.

A company outside of D.C. was my first client. I developed a direct import program for them and eventually took one of the owners to Colombia to introduce him to some of my contacts. I had been traveling south for years now and didn't give much thought to the anxiety a first visit can bring or the complexities of managing cross-cultural relationships. This wholesaler loved the trip and was convinced he needed to buy direct but felt he couldn't go back there himself or if he would understand the importation processes of those times.

"I'll buy everything from you," he told me one morning. "You mark it up a little and you can have all my business."

I thought, "*Wow, this is a solid marketing plan. I get to share my experiences with wholesalers in rural America, take them to Colombia, scare the s$%@ out of them, and have them give me all their business....um, yeah, done.*"

I started buying for several businesses around the U.S. and rented an apartment in Miami so I could be there in the middle of the night or whenever a shipment was cleared. I would make *sure* my customers got exactly what they needed or at least knew if a quality problem existed before they received the products in their warehouses. Knowing about a problem before you receive it allows you to make better decisions timelier.

My tenure in Miami staying knee-deep in importing gave me a fresh, in-depth look into the processes that I had prior only set up and let others manage my shipments. It's much easier to send all flowers to one location, but when you have multiple clients, you have to make sure everything gets to the different trucking companies and airlines required. My work would often be in the middle of the night, receiving shipments and printing labels for each box. I used a cargo agency in Doral, FL, right by the airport to clear and handle my flowers. The owner and I spent many nights on the loading docks unloading and loading trucks.

During down times, we goofed off like all dock workers would, but at a different level. He was a little older than I and drove a $100,000 Porsche 911 (a lot of money in those days) while I had a brand-new Corvette. He would make fun of my poor man's sports car when I parked next to him, I would poke fun at how little car he got for his money since a Porsche is a much smaller car. It all led to 2 a.m. races around the parking lots and buildings. We once did a donut competition that I naturally won. His Porsche crushed my little 'Vette in the many drag races we had, but we came up with other little tests of performance where I won a few but lost most. I always said the moment you drive off the lot with a brand-new Corvette, you know you have a used Chevy and after a few months it will creak, shake, and make noises. I loved the car but it caused me way too much trouble.

One day, I came into the office of my cargo agency and asked where my friend the owner was.

"He is going to be on vacation for nine to twelve months depending on good behavior," the accounting guy told me. Apparently, flowers were not *all* he was shipping.

I never saw or spoke to him again. I don't know what happened to him and his cargo agency closed after a few more months. You just never know who you are really dealing with in this business. I have a lot of friends in the industry, but I'm rarely surprised anymore by what I see or hear.

One Valentine's Day shipping period I was working in Miami, and at the end of the week I drove home in the 'Vette as usual. I got pulled over on the Florida turnpike by a drug enforcement unit of the Palm Beach County Sheriff's Office in an unmarked car. Back in those days, you got out of your car to greet an officer ready with your license and registration. Oh how things have changed!

"The reason I'm stopping you is you were exceeding the speed limit, you passed me and I was doing 55 miles per hour," the cop told me. He said he was with the drug enforcement department and asked if I knew how many drugs were traveling up and down the Florida Turnpike.

"No sir, but I can imagine it's a lot," I replied.

He asked where I was heading, I said, "Home." He asked where I was coming from, I said, "Miami." He asked what I was doing in Miami, I said, "Working." He asked what I did for a living, I said, "Importer." Naturally he asked what I imported and from where. I said, "Flowers from Colombia."

So now, he has a young 30-year-old in a new Corvette who imports from Colombia. I mentioned that it must "sound bad." The officer was very professional and asked if I had any drugs or large sums of money in my car. I said, "No sir."

He asked if I had any weapons. Hmmmm…this was not going to be good. "Yes sir I have a .45 in the glove compartment and there is a .380 on my ankle," I answered.

Things got pretty tense after that and backup arrived. "Okay, I want you to stand completely still," he told me. "I'm going to take the gun off your ankle, I'm warning you—*do not move.*"

I felt a tremble in my knees. He got my gun, backed up, and asked, "Do you mind if we search your vehicle?"

"No sir, please help yourself," I replied, trying to sound calm instead of nervous.

His backup had arrived with its K9 unit and they were ready to make a big bust. The officers searched the vehicle, ran my weapons permit, and ran the gun's serial numbers. While we were waiting for all this, the tension melted away and we chatted about all the cool things they've procured when stopping people on the turnpike. They were great guys, actually. In the end they gave me my guns, license, etc., and off I went.

You might be wondering why I had a permit to carry a gun. Besides being young and cool, driving my sports car, living in Miami, and traveling to Bogota like—yes, you guessed it—*Miami Vice*—I'd had some scary run-ins and felt self-defense was not a laughing matter. The drug wars were still going on and there were nightly murders in Miami by dealers. Sometimes gun fights even broke out in shopping malls. Again, no one was looking for me, but many innocent bystanders were caught in random gun violence, even in the 90s. I wasn't looking for trouble, but I knew I didn't want to be stuck hiding in the backroom of a store from a shooter with nothing to protect myself or my family.

I had learned much from a Winn Dixie store reset I did at 17 in Palm Bay, Florida. There a gunman killed multiple people in the store, including a few workers hiding in the store's backroom. The back doors were locked, and they were trapped. On a side note, after tear gas was deployed to flush out the shooter – the plants and flowers were no longer good, so we did a full reset of the floral department. The entire store was a bio or chem hazard and had to be reset. It was a sad and interesting process.

Back to carrying a gun – I was also asked a few times by grower friends of mine to go pick up money owed by their customers since I was in Miami. I picked up a bag once and found out later it had $10K in cash which was a lot back then. My assumption at the time was the money represented payments on flower sales from the farm, but in retrospect I had no way of knowing.

CHAPTER ELEVEN: The Commercial and Personal Pitfalls of a Perishable Industry

The Soviet Union collapsed in 1991 and the years afterward saw a resurgence of Russian black market or mafia dealers who bought roses from Ecuador and sometimes Miami. Roses would go for as much as $10.00 a stem for International Women's Day, a large holiday celebrated in Russia, so it was quite disruptive to the U.S. market. Russians would often pay with bags full of U.S. dollars and every grower wanted a piece of this business. They would pay $1.00 to $2.00 a stem with cash, an unheard of amount. The Russian mafias got a feel for capitalism by selling off former Soviet military equipment to the governments and the narcos in Colombia and Ecuador, then buying flowers among other things to sell back in the new Russia.

There was a particular Russian gentleman who I never formally met but often saw at trade shows in Ecuador, Colombia, and New York City, as well as occasionally at an importer's office in Miami. I never had a word with him, but his gray hair, hard eastern European facial features, and bright flower-patterned shirts stood out and were very recognizable.
One afternoon in Miami I had a lunch meeting in South Beach. I parked a few blocks over and started walking to Collins Avenue when I noticed a commotion down an alleyway. As I looked into the alley, I saw the Russian guy, who I immediately recognized, with another man beating a third guy to the ground. I kept walking faster, hoping he

didn't see me. I had my gun on me and one thing I learned about carrying is to walk away and walk *fast*. You don't want to get in an altercation and have the gun exposed because then it becomes a fight to see who can get control of it faster. Being shot with your own gun—well, I imagine that would not look cool. Flowers are a tough industry, and there is a lot going on in the U.S. and abroad with their various morals, ethics, and laws. It's not all rosy, pun intended again.

Consulting and selling to companies in several states and cities kept me busy flying around to farms and customers. I was living in Miami part time, then returning home on weekends to be with my wife and kids. My old company was starting to feel the effects of big corporate consolidations of buying power. "Going corporate," they called it. We had lost some of our Central Florida business to corporate deals, and regional players were disappearing nationwide. Since I sold a lot of flowers to my old company, we had a very good relationship, plus we were quasi-family or former family. I didn't know what we were, but in the South they call it "kinfolk."

There was a large company in the floral industry, USA Floral Products, Inc., which started by merging six large companies together in what they called a "roll-up." The idea was six companies can dominate together as the biggest company instead of six smaller companies fighting against each other. The man who had done a roll-up of the office supply stores and took them public wanted to try his hand at the floral industry.

Like a flash in the flashiest pan he was a success and then gone. He fell victim to the notion that flowers would be easier than office supplies and that an Ivy League education could trump a homegrown industry of people like me who started from the beginning, many with nothing.

The floral industry is particularly tough because it is perishable by its very nature. Flowers come from different countries at different quality levels depending on seasons and geography. Unlike the produce industry, there are no regulations or standards. You don't eat flowers and your idea of beauty or value is your own. It is a purchase about *emotion and impulse*, not necessity. And unlike the office supply business, if you make a bad purchase such as too many pencils or paper, you can't just put it on the shelf and sell it off over time. With flowers, if you buy too many—more than you can sell or the market can accommodate—you must throw them away and take a big loss. If you sell the blooms cheap just to get rid of them, you trigger a supply price war which is hard to overcome.

For example, if I have 200,000 roses in my cooler at a fair price but another importer sells them $0.15 cheaper, I don't have any choice but to sell mine $0.17 cents cheaper or I get left holding the bag and throwing away my roses. I can't hold my roses and wait until the market goes back up. Now, imagine 50 other importers doing the same thing – it takes only *one guy* to start a spiral of the market and we all lose. This happens every day, and it makes the flower market a challenge outsiders have taken for granted and failed at over and over again.

I used to consult for companies on their Valentine's Day purchases alone. Knowing what percentage to pre-book versus what percentage to buy on the open market was something only a person with a finger on Colombia and Ecuador's floral industry pulse could do well. Price is greatly affected by whether or not Ecuador's crop is early or Colombia's crop is late, with 10 to 20 other combinations of the most basic crop data.

It was one of the issues USA Floral was about to face, and in actuality their recklessness would kick off a series of pricing wars. Everyone without huge lines of credit to survive were getting taken out. We were all feeling this pressure and many of us could see it coming. I had a good friend, Dario, who was on the board of USA Floral. His Miami company had been acquired for $50 million dollars and now he sat on the board but he still owned his farms in Colombia. A roll-up scheme is only successful if it continues its acquisition strategy or it sells out to venture capital or enjoys so much critical mass and savings by sharing expenses from all companies that it totally dominates an industry. The result – more companies were getting searched out.

I went to Colombia to meet with Dario, learn why he sold his company, and see if it was right for my old company to join the roll up. He would provide a critical voice in deciding if we wanted to throw our hat in the ring. We decided to move forward and I went back to my old boss, asking if he wanted to join the roll-up. We made an agreement, so I called Dario to throw our hat in and get his support. The next six months were lawyers and accountants digging through all the books followed by completion of the acquisition and integration into the larger group. My old boss made a killing and I didn't do too bad myself for a young high school drop-out with international connections. I brokered my first multi-million dollar deal to a nearly $1 billion dollar floral conglomerate.

Since I had left my old company and enjoyed leading a successful consulting and import brokerage firm, things didn't change much for me. A few of my customers had sold out to this monster firm, and at first I was fearful of losing my business since the larger group would now do the buying and get deals for all their divisions. I was thankfully wrong. My business was booming as USA Floral was so busy buying new companies and taking the company public they couldn't handle the integration of their recent business purchases. With their new buying power and ownership of the best import companies in Miami, they should have and intended to improve the margins in all the regional companies they purchased. But they failed to focus internally and spent millions focused on being a publicly held company instead of a powerhouse floral company. In fact, their entire scheme was blossoming into a chaotic mess.

I learned a few things about roll-ups and big business during this time.

The first lesson was that once it was a publicly-traded company, I could read all their financial information online at Hoovers and the U.S. Securities and Exchange Commission (SEC). I downloaded and dug into every aspect of their business, noticing trends and benchmarks I had never seen before. My competitors now had their pants down and I could see it *all*. I also learned a roll-up really *wasn't* about improving a market, it was about being the only one *left in a market*.

These guys did nothing to integrate and improve their business operationally, as their new master was the stock market and analysts. They made decisions to move the needle on stock prices, *not* to improve the business. Most of the acquisitions were paid out in 50 percent cash and 50 percent stock in the company. There were six-month restrictions on owners selling their stock which meant that every six months former owners were selling off as much stock as they could causing stock prices to plummet with every sale. Because some acquisitions occurred at different times, sellers were dumping their stock every three to six months which kept executives scrambling to please market analysts, leaving room for me to sneak in the back door and sell their operating divisions a *lot* of flowers. I made so much money for a few years that I bought a big house on a private spring-fed lake, had an office in a separate wing, and hired a good CPA friend of mine, Drew, to handle the influx of business.

Drew and I would roll into the office adjacent to my home around 8 a.m. each day, fix some coffee, then head out back to the lake and do our morning slalom skiing before hitting the real work. Nothing like a little workout before work each day! Drew had come from big corporate America as a CFO so this was all new to him, but we worked hard and enjoyed our breaks when we could. Most afternoons we would look out the window at the lake and if it was glassy, one of us would say, "Wanna ski?"

There were three of us in the office, so when anyone heard "Wanna ski?" ears would perk up and the office's back door couldn't open fast enough. There was me, Drew, and my yellow lab, Buddy. If Buddy heard "Do you wanna ski?" it was on. He ran for the boat, jumped in, and waited on the bow. We would zip across the lake to a slalom course that was set up, with Buddy's ears flapping in the wind and his nose working overtime to take in the "Smells of Summertime, Lake Edition." Drew and I skied all summer and most of the winter, and made several trips to the Cayman Islands to scuba dive/ do accounting work. In the winter we went skiing in Colorado.

Those years were as good as it got—what more could we ask for?

Business has always had ups and downs. We were starting to finally see some movement in the big conglomerate USA Floral, and they were seeing me cherry-pick their companies, supplying the smaller regional companies they acquired with products some of their other acquisitions from the group could provide. At first, I lost a few deals, but then it turned into a battle for the business – me against their own company. I won some and lost some, and I remember the biggest battle was in regards to my old company. A guy from the USA Floral came to town to visit from said old company, my biggest customer at the time. Since I was the largest supplier, I showed up to meet him. We had a pleasant meeting and walked to the warehouse together. Then he hit me with his 'realization' – he didn't see his company buying from me anymore and I needed to be prepared.

Now, I've been threatened before and responded directly, "I understand your position and the needs of your company but you'll need to understand mine. I sell all my products to this company and they sell them to my old supermarket customers who, by the way, I hold great relationships with and meet with weekly. I'm telling you if your orders stop, I will start selling there and quickly you will realize the company you bought in Orlando with ties into its supermarket customers…I will take them all."

It was like a Mexican standoff. I'm pretty sure we were shooting at each other, metaphorically-speaking anyway. What unfolded over the next two years was they did, in fact, stop buying from me, and I did start selling to their customers. They closed my old company and months later I lost my customers to a corporate program which USA Floral got. I thought, *"Wow, he got me in the end."* One year later USA Floral imploded under its own weight and filed for bankruptcy after becoming the first $1 billion dollar floral company in history. *"Haha, I won!"* I thought. But did I *really?*

Since USA Floral owned many of my customers as I picked them apart, guess who got burned in the bankruptcy? They owed me hundreds of thousands of dollars when they filed and I never saw a *dime*. I spent two years paying off growers from whom I had bought the products. Not only did I lose a lot of money, I lost a huge chunk of my customer base. Now I was working twice as hard for half as much and sending anything I made to pay off past invoices to the farms I needed the most to continue going forward.

While all of this was going on, I had to let my good friend Drew, the CFO of my company go. There just was not enough work for both of us. It was a tough decision since I had lured him away from a safe, comfortable corporate job, but there was little choice.

I think only business owners understand the responsibility that comes with hiring someone. That hiree and their family relies on your success as much as you do. It can be a heavy burden; this experience gave me my first dose of employee responsibility and it was particularly hard because he was my friend.

So the business went on struggling as a one-man band for another year, just brokering to a handful of customers while paying down these farms. My friend Drew, who I had to let go, found out he had stage 4 cancer only a few months after I let him go. He had been finding it hard to get a job, his family was under tremendous stress, and now *this*?

Things had gotten pretty low at this point – my business was struggling and my friend was dying. His struggle was harder than mine, but I got to spend another year with him saying goodbye. We still did things together in between his hospital visits. And while we didn't ski anymore, we went to Orlando Magic and hockey games when he was up to it. I took him to doctor and chemo appointments when his wife had conflicts or just needed a break. Spending that time together was a blessing to me. We truly never know how close we feel to someone until their days are numbered. Because we loved the water so much, we had his ashes poured into a concrete artificial reef and dropped off the coast of Ft. Lauderdale. He's resting in peace there today, and I think of him often.

CHAPTER TWELVE: Working With the 'Marts', New Deals, and Trimming Company Fat

As I dug myself out from under the debts the conglomerate left me holding, I found new business as many people do. I've learned one can rise from the lowest point and find alternate work if driven enough. Having a wife and two kids is certainly a *huge* motivator, one that always pushed me to succeed. My beautiful wife had a career larger than mine when we met and gave it up to stay home and raise our kids. It was a huge sacrifice for her and one that paid off tenfold so it was my turn to hold up my end. Both my kids have passed my level of education – not in that it was a hard feat to outlast me in the school system, but they are both college-educated. I can't believe it, and I'm so thrilled for them and my wife for their efforts. My family is who I am most proud of.

Looking to make money fast prompted me to sell to Kmart – another big, solid company at the time. Again, what could *possibly* go wrong? I'd paid off the farms from the last financial fiasco and now had a full packaging facility in Orlando with 10 to 15 employees who were making it all happen. Business was booming between Kmart and my other import and consulting activities. No more roll-up scheme customers with crazy, out-of-control spending. Two years into having good ol' dependable Kmart as a client, they filed bankruptcy and again I was left holding the bag.

As I looked once more for ways to make money quickly, a grower in Colombia who had asked me to join him a few years earlier reached out. Having started my first business back then, the timing just wasn't right. Post-Kmart, however? The timing was *definitely* right as Kmart had filed for bankruptcy and again I was knocked down.

I merged my company with the Colombian's and became President of North American Operations for a five-farm group of over 600 acres in Bogota. My first task was to make sense of their Miami operation which was losing more money than I had ever seen a company lose and still survive. The single largest problem regarding most flower companies at the time was owners taking more money than the businesses could afford. It was my first company with a board of directors, and I immediately saw there was a huge overhead of executives suffocating the company. The office was on the Doral Country Club, the golf course now known as the Trump Doral. Everyone had an assistant who actually did most, if not all of the work. The company had over $350k invested in helping a small technology company develop an ERP solution for floral importers. There was *a lot* to chew on here on a larger scale than I had experienced thus far in my career.

My second task involved reorganizing a layer of management and supporting junior managers responsible for marketing, procurement, and bookkeeping. My third task concerned the IT systems. We had a full-time tech support service and 15 computers infected with every kind of malware one could imagine. The problem was so widespread, some employees called in each morning to ask a coworker to start their computer so it would be ready by the time they arrived. I spent many nights at the beginning of my tenure not on the loading docks, but in the office cleaning these machines so we could operate efficiently. From every avenue this was a clean-up of a poorly-run company and its core issues were only starting to become clear.

Every company I've ever consulted for had a list of customers who weren't paying. The key to collections is putting customer service first and negotiations second. Honey attracts more flies than vinegar, right? This company had one particular customer who owed us a lot of money. In an effort to collect it, I got on a flight to Colorado where I could sit with the customer and determine what could be done. After learning this company had lost a major account and was drowning in overhead, I developed a strategy. Here we had a (basically) good group of people who built an empire around a large amount of business from two main sources, and one of those had dropped off. I had witnessed this many times on various levels, and this one was huge.

After analyzing their business, I knew what needed to be done to save the jobs of the employees, the relationships with customers, and the money owed to the company for whom I worked. We would do a hybrid acquisition requiring a drastic reduction of infrastructure and expenses. Because there were leases, contracts, and commitments, the hybrid project was difficult for the company. All these problems were not *my* problems, so the simple solution for me and what made it a hybrid was – opening a new company, hiring the workers needed, and putting the business in a smaller location scaled to a profitable size. In hybrid situations, we shed all the old expenses and payables which were not part of our new company going forward.

The result? Employees kept their jobs and the owner stayed to manage operations. Customers never saw a blip in service, and we expanded our operations out west, making everyone happy. The board at my new company called it "Doing a Denver" and continually asked when we could do another.

The largest new customer in this transaction was Sam's Club, a division of Walmart. It was naturally the biggest customer of my career at that juncture, as well as a complex vendor managed program that paid every time one of our flowers went through the register, also called a pay-per-scan program.

I marveled at the level of technology available to vendors through Walmart and Sam's Club. I could log into their system and see our inventory in each store, including whenever a flower ran through the register. For all of the faults of which Walmart is accused, I must say they were my favorite customer. The company provided reports detailing our products' sell-through and shrink rates. Basically, our product sold on its own merit. If we lost the business, it was because our products didn't sell, not because someone decided to buy elsewhere – on most fronts, anyway.

Several months after taking over the business, we were exhibiting at a national trade show for supermarkets. It was going to be my first opportunity to meet with the buyer for Sam's Club, a feisty lady who possessed the "old school Walmart" mentality which often gave the corporation a bad name. She stopped by our booth at the trade show, we exchanged pleasantries and agreed to go meet in a private conference room. We walked together having a pleasant conversation about the show and the floral business. I was excited to meet her and it all seemed to be going well. Then we sat down in the conference room, and she looked me dead in the eye and demanded, "You have 15 minutes to tell me why I shouldn't throw you the hell out of all my stores. What makes you think you can just come in and buy my business?"

Boom – I'll never forget those words! There it was, spoken directly with a high level of pent-up resentment. Fortunately for me it was not an uncommon supermarket floral buyer management persona. Many supermarket floral buyers have *huge* egos and think because they work for *huge* companies they can take out their insecurities on their vendors. Since this was not my first rodeo, I jumped right in. I thanked her for the opportunity to meet with her, and made it very clear I would never try to buy her business. I came into this relationship with the best intentions of helping our friends in Denver, to better support Sam's Clubs and to help avoid potential job loss of the people who understand the Clubs best.

I shared my vision for supporting the clubs. I explained our new ability as a large grower in Colombia and how we would be able to better serve her needs. I took the wind right out of her seriously puffed-up sails, when she believed I was going to cave or collapse.

"I had every intention of throwing you out of all my stores today," she remarked 30 minutes into our conversation. She also mentioned that she appreciated my time and would allow us to continue serving her stores less the 30 percent she was going to take back and give to another vendor. Clearly another supplier had gotten in her ear prior to my meeting and planted the seed that I had bought her business. She had bitten and to save face she felt she had to take 30 percent of the stores to demonstrate her authority.

I left the meeting pretty happy overall, but I remember telling someone in the meeting with me, "She will be gone from Walmart in the next six months." Her style of management was not the direction I'd seen from Walmart to date. Sure enough, a short time later she was gone.

My last meeting with her was in Bentonville, AR, the headquarters for Walmart. The day before the meeting Hurricane Charley was bearing down on my home in Florida so I called the buyer and asked if we could reschedule, as I needed to prepare for the storm and my wife and kids needed my help. She responded, "You asked for this appointment if you can't make it then don't ask for another." It was this type of buyer who gave the company such a bad name.

I went to the meeting, but kept in contact with my wife who

was preparing as best she could for the storm. She actually had me buy a generator in Arkansas since they were sold out in Florida. I arrived back in Orlando around midnight with a generator coming out on the luggage belt and it was obvious many people wished they could take it. Orlando International Airport closed two hours later; I had barely made it back home. We lost part of our roof during the hurricane storm and spent eight days without power making the generator worth its weight in gold.

Starting a new project brings unknown circumstances that remain unseen until well into it. Working for the Colombians was no different. Coming into the organization, the goal was to sell more flowers. Now having Sam's Clubs and Safeway Supermarkets as customers from the Denver deal, it became clear four weeks in that the farms didn't have the production to handle the new business or the energy to supply the new business.

When doing a deal, whether it be a transaction or a new job, it's important to understand the motivations of all parties involved. The farms had a Colombian sales manager who had no interest in giving the production to an internal company because he wanted to sell the production himself. It was an immediate conflict with competing personalities and one of the main reasons their Miami company that I now ran was such a mess before I got there.

As we struggled to get flowers needed in Denver for the new operation there seemed to be something else going on behind the scenes in Colombia. The farms were having currency issues as they converted dollars to pesos through the central bank. For every million dollars going in converting to pesos then back to dollars meant only $750,000 came back out. The farms were literally losing money on currency exchanges plus one farm had water shortages causing it to lose money operationally. On top of those issues, some genius had the idea to invest a few million dollars in computerized and automated fertilization injection systems to cut one great benefit a farm in South America had – low wages. It was clearly backfiring.

Aside from business issues with this large, growing operation there were personality issues with its ownership. The reason we could not get the flowers we needed from our own farms was because Juan, the sales manager in Colombia, got commissions only on the products he sold. To sell to an inner company division precluded him from his commission money. So, the fight was on once again. Juan bucked the system at every turn, claiming to get better prices from other parts of the world or stripping colors from assortments knowing we couldn't sell the balance. We could buy flowers easier, faster, and cheaper from other farms than from our own company thanks to Juan. Being in Colombia day in and day out Juan had the direct ear of the owners and made life difficult.

Being the boss is a tough job that only those who have been a boss or owner can truly understand. The stresses of running a business, employee issues, payroll, supply, demand, customers, and accounting make taking vacations difficult. During this time, I took my family to Hawaii for a vacation. Yes, I know poor me, things are tough. The entire time I was gone Juan was trying to take my job in the U.S., by getting the business in the U.S. shut down and moving the operation to Colombia where he could control it.

About a year into this job, I came into my office in Miami one day and found the bank accounts had been drained. I put in a call to Colombia to see if they knew anything about it. There was no response. The following day passed with emails and calls to Colombia about the bank accounts. There was no response. I sent emails regarding normal business and received immediate responses as they continued to ignore my emails and calls about the bank account.

A few more days passed without resolution, money would come into the account from clients but disappear at night without paying suppliers, so I decided to go home early to Orlando and work the problem. I had a call with my attorney for some advice on how to handle the situation. As an officer of the U.S. corporation, I had concerns about what was happening. My attorney's advice was since I had no idea who took this money, it could have been the U.S. federal government. He suggested I resign immediately in protest before I woke up one morning and found I was the president of a U.S. money laundering operation for a Colombian company. Attorneys get paid to think the worst or maybe they think the worst so they get paid more. I took his advice and sent my resignation.

I had growing suspicions about this group of growers. First, there was one farm I wasn't allowed to visit. It had a private landing strip and required a small private plane. I was told the area was not safe and that after landing there was a 30 minute window to get back in the air before the people who saw the landing came to the farm to see who had arrived. Rumors were the manager of the farm couldn't be trusted so they never told him when they were coming. Second, one of the growers who I had never met owned an island off the coast of Colombia and ran some boat services. I had plenty of reasons to let my attorney raise my suspicions. At the time almost all growers rode in bullet proof cars, yet my boss did not despite being one of the wealthiest growers in Colombia. I had never suspected him of being a narco trafficker but possibly a financier of a right wing paramilitary group working against the narcos which was a more likely capitalist move in the interest of his businesses.

A few months later I found out everything was on the up and up but the farms had financial issues and needed the cash to meet obligations. Six months later they closed Denver, then a few of the farms. There were bigger problems than I had seen initially. Eventually they closed the Miami operation as well.

In 1990 a large flower importer and major competitor of mine in the supermarkets was found stuffed in the trunk of his Buick Regal with multiple gunshot wounds down the street from my office. He was a former Israeli intelligence officer turned floral guy giving him a reason to be in Colombia. He was being investigated by 3 US government agencies including the secret service for his role in training paramilitary and narco traffickers in Colombia. He had warrants for his arrest in Colombia for involvement in the assassination of an anti drug-trafficking candidate for President of Colombia. Apparently he said too much to the wrong people and someone wanted him gone. You never know who you are doing business with in this industry.

CHAPTER THIRTEEN: Real Estate Adventures, Helping Another Floral Business Make Bank, Lots of Traveling and a Car Chase

After that chapter in my life I decided I really wanted to get out of the industry. The real estate industry was flying high and my lake house was worth a fortune, so we decided to sell the house and move out to the country. After meeting with a few realtors, I decided to go straight to the source, which is how I handle most things. I went and got my real estate license. It was the first time I had been back to school for anything since 10th grade, and I *loved* it. We sold the house and made a bunch of money near the top of the market but then thought, *"Well, where do we live now?"*

Housing was (and is) expensive, and who wants to roll profits into a high priced home that might fall when the real estate bubble bursts? We decided after visiting some family in North Florida we would move out to the country, pay cash for a home, and live a simpler life. I was burnt out on the importing industry and convinced I was a real estate genius after selling my own home. Apparently, I was not.

The market started collapsing nationwide, the bubble had burst and one of the hardest financial crises hit the U.S. It resulted in a two-year sabbatical which I spent enjoying my family with no real bills piling up. It was just a good time to relax, raise some chickens, grow a garden, and teach the kids how to play outdoors. We lived a pretty highfalutin' lifestyle back in Central Florida, but these were simpler days in Northwest Florida only three miles from the Alabama border.

Soon I was back to consulting for companies that needed import and supermarket experience, as well as companies that wanted to buy and sell their businesses. Buying or selling another person's business in Florida requires a real estate brokers license, which I had. I worked with a few companies in Miami, putting together buyers and sellers yet it was my experience in imports, technology, and supermarkets that prompted most companies to hire me.

I helped companies with their marketing, their computer systems, and their relationship building with customers and suppliers while also working to build a career outside of the floral industry. I was vacationing on the beach when I got a call from Ricardo, an old friend in Ecuador. He told me about this guy in San Francisco who was buying his company and another in Ecuador as part of a roll-up to go public. Where had I heard this before? He asked if I would fly to California and meet with this guy as he was looking for an operations man to oversee the acquisitions in Ecuador. It made sense that Ricardo wanted someone he knew involved in oversight of his newly-acquired company.

I took the meeting with a gentleman named Brent in California and was immediately impressed with his story, his vision, and the uniqueness of his business plan. Plus, I saw an opportunity to have pre-IPO shares of a company. Even if it failed, I could make some quick cash. Like all the companies that I consult or work for, there is always more to the story than what is evidenced up front, and this one would become a 10 year learning experience full of challenges and hardships but also invaluable learning experiences that I don't regret to this day.

Day one of working I was supposed to fly to Los Angeles, meet with some suppliers, and see our distribution center in Southern California. Afterwards, I was to drive up the coast to San Francisco hitting suppliers all the way. Also, on day one, I was to let go an employee in Miami whom I had never met, never having yet to set foot in the facility which was now under my responsibility. I hopped off the plane at LAX, called down to the employee in Miami, and advised them of their exit from the company and severance package. It was going to be an interesting company and project.

The company had millions in sales but a payroll that equaled its sales. There were facilities in four cities and three states plus the two new farms in Ecuador. It was one of those build-it-and-they-will-come projects I had only heard of and never seen. The floral industry at the time was a bootstrap, a self-fund-insider-run industry where one either made money and continued or lost money and went out of business. The concept of losing money for years while building or growing through acquisition didn't make sense to me at the time.

My role in this business kept me in the air traveling among the growers on the West Coast, the office in Miami, as well as in Colombia and Ecuador and in the HQ office in San Francisco. I usually rolled out on Sunday night to be in San Fran or Miami Monday morning, and went home late on Friday.

Traveling full time is something anyone has to get used to and in the beginning it was exciting. Every business unit, supplier, or customer was new and everything was full of opportunity. I worked all day and most nights in my hotel rooms, as you are never more productive than when you are working on a new project and have air/hotel time to dot all the I's and cross all the T's. They got their money's worth out of my time for sure.

After a year I began to grow weary of the extensive travel and dread started to set in. I couldn't wait to get home to the family, and dreaded leaving Sunday night, so I would put it off until Monday morning. After a few months of that, I went numb. Traveling became so routine I was neither tired or excited, I just did it. it. I had a flight attendant tell me she knew I traveled a lot, she said I had "that stare" – everything blocked out and in thought somewhere else. With extensive travel, I didn't share the concern or excitement of occasional travelers. There was no wondering where I was going, where I was parking, or how to get through security. I parked on the same floor every time in the same parking lot of the same airline. I was a platinum member with hotels and airlines and got to the airport and headed for the executive club for my morning breakfast and cup of coffee. Once I hit status back in the day, every flight was a free upgrade to first class. It was like walking on a treadmill each morning with none of the challenges of other travelers. I never checked a bag so no bag ever got lost. On the rare occasion I actually checked a bag it was 'priority' and always came down the belt first.

I remember once getting up early Monday morning (as usual) around 3 a.m. to hit the shower, grab some clothes, and take off to the airport. As I was going through security and took off my shoes, the TSA guy looked down and said, "Really? Your wife's socks?"

I looked down and sure enough – I saw these panty-hose-looking socks on my feet – a result of trying to get dressed in the dark. On another trip to Chicago in winter, I accidentally packed my wife's winter coat. When I left the Chicago airport it was 10 degrees as I pulled out my coat. It resulted in a big man, tiny coat situation – the sleeves came down barely past my elbows. Pretty funny until I had to return to the airport and buy a $400 coat just to get to my meetings.

Because of time changes I could fly to LA, have a lunch meeting and fly back to Orlando on the same day. I once had a meeting in Santa Barbara that was canceled while I was in flight so I booked a flight back while in the air, landed, went to the sky lounge, had lunch and caught the next flight back home.

In a two week period of travels, I experienced three natural disasters. I was sitting at my desk in the hotel in San

Francisco one night and things began to shake back and forth like the building was on rollers. It was an earthquake – something I had never experienced. Later that same week, I flew down to Ecuador and was diverted on a drive to Banos because a lava flow from Mt. Tungurahua had just erupted. It took me three additional hours traversing the mountains to reach Banos that night. Even then parts of the roads were covered in hardened ash from past lava flows. I drove over the flows with rooftops and street signs poking through the hardened lava, plus the dust on everyone's headlights along the detour made the roadway nearly impossible to see. When I arrived back in Orlando for the weekend, there was a close brush with Hurricane Irene off the coast of Florida so I stayed home the following week and enjoyed some peaceful time with the family. While they make for interesting stories, international travel can be challenging, sometimes you just need to decompress at home with the ones you love.

During my early years in Ecuador, before friends or an established company, I used to hire a car to visit the farms much like my early days in Colombia. When I couldn't find a private driver I took taxis which was usually more difficult because my Spanish, while better, was still limited. To reach the farms far away from the city I would have to ask how far a taxi was willing to take me. To get to farms in Riobamba or Banos took five hours, which meant a three-hour taxi ride to the small town of Ambato where the taxi would drop me off and then I would have to find another taxi to finish the additional two hours. It was like the pony express from a wild west movie. I would get to Ambato with everyone staring at me, I'd try to find something to eat then look for a source of transport to Banos. By car it was another two hours, but if I was forced to take the bus which looked terrifying on those mountain roads, it might take five to six hours if nothing went wrong. Two buses on those back roads often resulted in one having to back up down the mountain to allow another to pass. These were very skilled drivers but I saw more than one flipped over or stuck in the mud. Plus, I was still sensitive from being in Colombia where buses, especially with an American on them, were not safe.

Today I rarely travel so I feel the pains of many occasional travelers. I don't belong to the clubs and I don't get free upgrades to first class. Because of my past travels, I am a lifetime platinum member of a hotel chain and still gold at the car rental agency, but other than that I'm humping it through the airport sipping the same burnt coffee as everyone else hoping to get a seat with a power port at the gate. When traveling in South America now I rent a car or take an Uber, the service new to Ecuador only in the last few years. Today in Colombia and Ecuador I feel safer than if I were in Detroit.

As this new project progressed, I learned more and more of the plans and the CEO's vision as well as what he did well…and not so well. For me it was a great experience because I knew what he didn't, and he knew what I didn't.

One of the highlights of my time working under this CEO and board was an opportunity at an all-company meeting. I was going to make a presentation to the entire company, but more importantly the Chairman of the Board who was also a Chairman for Loreal, the Gap, and other big, big companies. It was my time to shine and I worked for weeks on my PowerPoint presentation which was going to knock his socks off. On the day of the meeting I sat through other executives' presentations in anticipation of mine. There were some great presentations, but I felt I fared very well against my counterparts. I was set to present after lunch break and after two others.

I got up and started ripping through the talking points on why my division was going to be the future of this company and what we had already accomplished as an industry leader. I got positive feedback and participation from everyone in the room, and was convinced the Chairman was equally impressed. I looked over at him and he had nodded off, sleeping in his chair. I was laughing to myself; *"Way to go Buddy, you really lit the world on fire."* I kept going, finished the presentation, and got my kudos. It was an awesome experience since public speaking is something everyone has to work at, but how ironic my biggest speech *ever* put the man to sleep. I still chuckle about it sometimes.

As the project progressed, things started looking dim. The world economy was beginning to see some pressures, markets were starting to decline, and businesses were struggling to keep capital. This world disorder started during the Arab spring uprisings This company was supposed to go public in London, and the main contributor to this process had fallen below a required capital reserve to legally fund the IPO. Alternatives were sourced, vetted, and entertained while I remained focused on running the operations of the core business, at least from the supply side. There was an entire team in San Fran and Boston focused on the eCommerce sector of the business in which I had yet to be exposed, but it was coming.

As the IPO failed there were an increasing number of unhappy investors, scared employees, and nervous suppliers. Money was tight, and it seemed like everyone and their dog was threatening lawsuits against the management and board members for the millions of investments made with no question of how it was being used. This company had a huge burn of cash each month and lived from investment to investment in anticipation of a mass payout during the IPO. Eventually an investor group took over the company and installed a temporary manager (receiver) to assess operations, make some quick cash-saving decisions, and recommend the next moves to the investors.

I was at home one weekend and I got a call from this new manager whom I had never met or spoken with. He introduced himself, shared a quick synopsis of his goals, and asked me to explain what my division did and where I was going with it. Game on, I quickly jumped up on a hickory stump and said boy let me tell you what.

After about 15 minutes of chatting, he said, "Okay, I really planned on cutting this division to save money, but I think what you're doing has merit and could be interesting to spend some more time analyzing."

He added that I needed to make cuts across the board and lay off three people from all the locations I controlled.

Since I had to tell him who the people were, I offered, "Okay, I'll get back to you by tomorrow afternoon with how and who I think we should proceed."

"No I meant right now, give me the three from each location you're going to fire right now," he replied.

Fortunately for me, my time as a consultant helping struggling companies get their businesses scaled with the absence of personal connections meant I knew *exactly* what he was doing. I quickly gave him the names, he thanked me and added, "Let them go Monday morning and enjoy your weekend. I want to see you in San Francisco next week, let me know when you plan to arrive." Click.

In the coming weeks the new investor manager and I spent a lot of time together looking at various aspects of the business, shutting down locations, and putting together short-term plans which allowed the investment group to put in more money to cover reduced expenses. Since we got along so well he was recommending me to be the new president going forward but met resistance from the former CEO and founder of the company. The former CEO wanted *his* CMO, who had been there since the beginning, to get this new leadership position.

The chairman of our new board of directors made a decision to make Chris, the CMO, and myself co-presidents of the company in a move clearly designed to see who would come out on top and be a better long-term CEO. I became co-president and COO in charge of operations, accounting, and finance, and Chris handled his duties as CMO and now co-president. We actually worked well together and spent several months teaching and learning each other's daily tasks.

I introduced Chris to our wholesale customers, and we spent a few days in Vegas at a vendor exhibition show in which we were participating. I did what I had always done with clients – I took him to South America to get a firsthand look at what I do. On a trip to Ecuador to see the office I had opened there we decided to stay over a weekend so he could see the sites of Ecuador as well. I even took him down to colonial Quito to see the old churches and the presidential palace.

There is often excitement when I'm in South America and this trip was no different. After walking up hills at an altitude of nearly 10,000 feet, we decided to grab a taxi. I threw my hand out and one of what seemed like a million yellow taxis pulled right up. Apparently, taxis are not allowed to stop on the road in the colonial part of Quito to pick people up, because a police officer standing on the corner behind us came running up to the window of the cab and started yelling at the driver.

The taxi took off with a jolt, the officer running behind us. As we looked back, he hailed his own taxi, jumped in, and the race was *on*. Our driver weaved in and out of cars, turned left, then right, then left again. He was putting on a hat, then taking it off trying to blend in with the other cabs. We were in a police chase down the streets of Quito, being thrown from one side of the cab to the other, all of it happening quickly. We got stuck behind traffic at a light with nowhere to go when I noticed the barrel of a gun come right by me and in the window at the head of the driver. We, well *he*, had been caught.

"Quick, let's bail!" I said to Chris.

We went out the back door on the opposite side and quickly ran down a few streets collecting our thoughts on what had just happened. I'd been to South America over 100 times, but that was my first car chase. It's always something new when you're traveling there!

We continued restructuring and reducing expenses to achieve the goals of the board to which we both reported. They had invested over 20 million collectively and we needed to raise *another four to five million* to continue operations and protect their equity in the company.

The only chance for them to see any money back was to help the company get profitable and sell it off at a later date. My job was to raise more capital, streamline operations, and grow new revenue sources. I had never raised capital but the other two functions were directly in my wheelhouse, so who better to do it? Chris was a brilliant ecommerce professional, but was not part of this floral industry and we both stayed in our own lanes. Part of the reduction of costs involved closing unprofitable locations and moving the corporate offices to the Mission District of San Francisco. Previously we were in the suburbs – a quick ride over the Golden Gate Bridge and then we were in a low rent section of the city across the street from a marijuana dispensary before it was even legal. Our staff loved the up-and-coming neighborhood close to public transportation where everyone came in wearing flip flops and carrying backpacks. I was more like a fish out of water with my blue blazer and dress shoes, driving a rental car, and carrying a briefcase. I always hated their work ethic coming in at 9:30 – 10:00 a.m. Pacific time, which was early afternoon in our Miami and Ecuador offices. But man, these people were talented. There is a lot to say about the creative expertise of people in California. I respected them very much.

I enjoyed working with the team, learning what they do and focusing my efforts on the business and the best interest of the investors/shareholders. While Chris and I got along very well and complemented each other's strengths and weaknesses, I had already learned business sometimes brings cruel gut punches. How one deals with them is critical to survival.

CHAPTER FOURTEEN: The Good CEO Fight and Why Organic isn't Always Best

The board had brought in a new member who had taken over as CEO from one of the companies we sold off after the failed IPO. Kathy was a strong executive who had been a CEO and CFO of a few large retail brands based in San Francisco. She was a very strong board member and a power puncher. She loved to rattle executives with direct, blunt accusatory statements during board meetings. She was an animal.

After a few board meetings I was convinced the board had brought her in to become the next CEO assuming it wasn't me or Chris.

I sat Chris down, shared my concerns, and said, "Listen, this lady is going to shred us unless we strike first. If one of us doesn't get behind the other and move to name a CEO she will be the next CEO and we will both be gone within two weeks."

We took a few days to talk and work through all of the functions of the business, each of our experience levels and concluded he would back me in a bid to be the next CEO. It was a tough decision for him, he was nearly a co-founder of the business having been there toward the beginning. But we both knew we were up against a killer and if one or both of us were to survive what I felt was coming, we had to make this change. We wrote out a brief statement on our plans to grow the business, how we were going to do it, and why we needed a clear leadership structure including me as CEO of the company.

The board received our communication and requested time to discuss internally. The fight was *on again.* Some wanted Kathy to take over as suspected. The chairman of the board wanted me to take over. The next board meeting was tough. I got grilled by everyone about my ability, my experience, my vision, and my leadership style, as well as why after being part of former management I should not be thrown out the door. It's rough at that level but I had been in similar combative meetings with the Colombians a few years earlier, the Sam's Club buyer, and others.

I was traveling a few weeks later and I got a call from the chairman who said, "I like your proposal and we want to move forward with you. I want you to consolidate offices on the East Coast where you can move quicker between offices."

He continued, "Set up an office in Orlando, hire a team, and start a plan to move everything. Keep it between you and I, we don't need an interruption to the business while you work this out. Oh and let Chris go tomorrow, we don't need him anymore, he's too expensive, and that'll give you better control over the transition." *Click.*

Normally I would have just followed through with this because he was effectively correct: financially and operationally it didn't make sense to have Chris involved. I couldn't lie to these people, so I went to bat for him the next day and told the chairman I needed Chris as a consultant for a period of time to help with a smooth transition. He reluctantly agreed and I had to work fast.

Everyone knew we were closing the offices in California; people were out looking for jobs and I had to quickly hire a team in Orlando that could handle ecommerce operations, which was the bulk of our business at that point. I pulled in a former business partner of mine who was an expert in ecommerce and tasked him with building out a team quickly and transitioning over the operations in a matter of weeks. With his help we pulled off a miracle – there was no drop in business revenue and all the financial improvements were accomplished in the matter of a few months.

The next board meeting came and I was ready to take my victory lap. Little did I know, Kathy-the-board-member hoping to take control of the company was unaware of the decision to close the California office and move to the East Coast. I couldn't see her on the call, but I could tell she had fire in her eyes as she immediately started ripping into me about when I was going to share my plan to gut an entire office of people and hire all new people in Orlando with the board? Did I understand the legal repercussions of my actions? What about being sued by the office leasing company, department of labor, etc., etc.?

She was all over me without a word spoken from the

chairman who directed me to do it. I think he just wanted to see how I handled it – would I step up or blame him and look for protection? I had been through this before with another board where a member came to town and wanted to take the entire staff out to a nice dinner. He ordered $500 bottles of wine and stuck me with the bill for over $3,000. At the next board meeting, members were asking me why entertainment expenses were so high, but there wasn't a peep from the board member.

I could take the heat. I stuck to my talking points, discussed the vision, showed the savings, and ended the call getting congrats from all of the board members, including Kathy. I weathered the control struggle and the board call. I'm a big believer in sticking to your plan, talking past the noise, and not worrying about fighting for your reputation. Do what is right and your reputation will speak for itself.

Many of the things I do as a consultant or corporate officer are tough. They often appear heartless but if they save money, save the company, and save jobs overall, they are necessary evils because going out of business doesn't help anyone. Everyone I have ever let go has gone on to another job. Many I still follow today who went on to have greater careers. In the case of this business, in addition to the investors that were in for millions, we had many farms owed a lot of money, including some of my friends in the floral industry. The cost cutting I had to do was to get the new investments necessary to pay those farms and keep as many people employed as possible.

As the former COO and now CEO, I became the voice of the company and our eco-lifestyle-based business model. The founder of the company was very much into organics and I had always been into the human rights of workers in farms who grew flowers and vegetables. I did my best to continue the mission of organic production while increasing the initiatives of worker benefits and sustainable production. Going organic really only affects the way a plant is grown, but does little to protect the environment around the farm or care for its workers. Using organic fertilizers on plants and allowing them to run into nearby streams can cause massive growths of hydrillas which disrupt the water's flow, killing animals and vegetation up and downstream. Spraying workers with organic concentrated fish emulation can burn the skin right off their bodies. Organic is not enough, it's just a growing technique and is *not* sustainable growing in and on its own.

I was also managing director of a sustainability fund investing in farms that want to grow organically. One day I was at a vegetable farm in which we had invested just outside of Gainesville, Florida. I was waiting for the farmer/owner to arrive. As I walked across the loading dock at the warehouse I noticed a cooler obviously not in service. It is not unusual to turn them off when it's not picking season. The door was propped open, likely to minimize mold in the cooler. I stuck my head in to see what it looked like and since there was no power I used the flashlight on my phone.

Inside this cooler with mold and mildew all over the floor and walls were six to eight beds made out of wooden pallets with blankets and pillows on top. This good-for-the-earth grower of USDA-certified organic produce was putting his illegal immigrant workers in the coolers to sleep and work the fields during the day.

I was floored thinking of all the upper middle income, health-conscious do-gooders shopping in their neighborhood Whole Foods thinking how great they are for buying organic produce. Yet they don't know anything about worker's conditions , only that organic is "good for the environment." It immediately brought me back to the days when my first boss died from toxic overexposure, as well as my friend, an American grower in Ecuador who had invented a vacuum system to manage pests in balance with mother nature and even offered 401k plans for workers. It also made me think of those in the industry like me who focused on sustainability as a business method where organic growing is included *but* not exclusive as a seal of approval.

The next five-plus years I spent promoting why sustainable floriculture is important and what the differences are in seals like Rainforest Alliance, USDA Organic, Fair Trade, Veriflora®, Florverde®, and others.

I was fortunate enough to have a direct-to-consumer platform via our website and social media to speak to consumers directly. I became an advocate for sustainable floriculture and did media whenever possible to educate shoppers on what I called "Choices that Matter" by looking for certification seals on products they buy. At the time there was a big movement in the U.S. toward lifestyles of health and sustainability. Shoppers wanted to know how their products were grown or produced by companies that cared about their workers and the environment. Every holiday I did interviews on CNN, Bloomberg, ABC, NPR, and any other TV or radio outlet that would have me. It taught me a great deal about reaching consumers and connecting on mutual issues.

I even worked with Al Gore in Boca Raton, FL, helping sponsor part of his book tour, *An Inconvenient Truth*. It was at this time that I realized – I can write a book too. Little did I know then that it would take me 10 years to finish this book.

After five years of promoting these seals and getting more and more involved in sustainability, I saw the industry become more about money than sustainability with everyone fighting for the almighty dollar. I served on the Sustainability Council for Veriflora®, and a council for converting Veriflora® into an ANSI- and eventually ISO-certified company on a global scale. After a week of meetings at the University of California Berkeley I realized how dysfunctional and money-hungry these organizations were. Getting them all together in a room to decide the key points of an international agreement was impossible. Everyone was fighting for their causes and the money it represented. Don't get me wrong, all of these causes are good causes and the standards of each are steps in the right direction, but it was time to leave the direct supporting role of these non-governmental organizations and focus on my own standards using these guidelines. Sustainability seals are a great way to ensure your suppliers or the products you buy stand for *something* but they are not the end all. We all have to be responsible for ensuring what we are truly buying the best we can and it all starts with getting a sense of the source of the person, company, product, and industry.

While I was managing director for the sustainability fund we were also invested in a USDA organic farm in Mexico. Coming into this after investments were made, I was tasked with assessing these troubled investments and determining if it was in the funds best interest to continue funding or to liquidate. Excited to learn as much as I could beyond memorizing stacks of investment documents, I hit the road to visit the farms.

The Mexico operation was in the middle of the desert in Baja Mexico. I flew into Cabo San Lucas and drove a few hours out into the desert where one would think nothing could grow to an heirloom tomato farm begun with a $1.2 M investment from the fund. I met the grower/owner, Ephraim. Ephraim was an Israeli citizen living part time in Mexico and San Diego.

It was a strange place to grow tomatoes in the desert since water was very scarce and there was nothing for about 100 miles. It seemed like a more likely place to grow something you needed to hide, but I didn't see anything indicating that was the case other than the oddity of a million dollar infrastructure sitting alone in the desert. After a pleasant day of touring the farm and discussing operations with Ephraim and various non-English speaking workers, I headed back to Cabo and a dinner meeting with Ephraim and his wife. I asked him to bring the financial documents to me so I could analyze the cash flow statements and anticipated needs. Instead, he brought me two months of bank statements.

I could see immediately we were playing cat and mouse, and I was apparently the rodent. At this juncture the fund had increased its investment and was now in for $1.4M. Ephraim *did not* want to show me where the money was spent, which was more than a little shady. He claimed they didn't have financial paperwork – just bank statements – so I requested two years of statements starting from the beginning of the funds' investment. I left town with the agreement that I would return in three weeks to review the requested materials.

Upon planning my return trip, Ephraim suggested we meet in San Diego because he wanted me to meet his partners. As I read through eight inches of agreements and legal documents, I found the name of one Mexican partner. It is not uncommon to have a national as a partner, but Ephraim said meet my *partners* so I was anxious to learn more. I flew to San Diego and we met at my hotel. In comes Ephraim with two men claiming to be his partners in the tomato farm. I later learned they were ex-military Israelis, and quizzed them on the Mexican partner named in the corporate charter and loan documents. They claimed to know nothing about the Mexican national named in the documents I had quickly shown them. They said, "Listen, we don't know who that is or where you got that, but we three own this farm and need additional investment from you or we will lose the crops currently in the ground.

Since this wasn't my first rodeo, I answered, "Listen. I don't know who you two are or why I'm not seeing copies of cash flow statements on how you spent our million dollars, but not another dime is coming until we get this straightened out."

"If you don't send us money you will forfeit your side of the partnership," they replied. I let them know if we couldn't get this figured out and the money accounted for we would start liquidating assets and selling off what our funds were used to buy.

They were *very clear* in letting me know if I returned to the farm I would "disappear in the desert." At that very moment I was thankful to be in San Diego. Whoever these two men were, they were big and intimidating.

I spent the coming weeks digging through documents, talking with attorneys to explore options in NYC, Mexico City, and San Diego. Mexican attorneys said "Well, they live in San Diego." U.S. attorneys noted the property was *in* Mexico and they were citizens of Israel. Basically I had no recourse and driving into the desert alone didn't feel like a prudent move.

I conveyed the challenges to the main investor of the fund, who said, "Robert, I really don't need this nonsense and the write off will probably benefit me more this year so just walk away from it instead of spending more money with lawyers or getting yourself killed by heading back to the farm.

He was right though I had never seen someone walk away from almost $2M and call it a good write-off.

During this period I had a vision to grow the business via acquisitions. Not a roll-up, but a strategic acquisition of companies that brought synergies, efficiencies, and economies of scale. I saw the business as an ecommerce enterprise that needed a brick and mortar customer base to improve its buying power and diversify the business model. I wanted to offer nationwide delivery of floral gifts to eco-minded consumers via online and instore purchases. I had a touch screen kiosk idea that could offer shoppers in supermarkets the ability to buy local and take flowers home or send flowers nationwide. Having the same products available to send nationwide in supermarkets exposed us to hundreds of thousands shoppers per store with the average supermarket at the time having 200 stores. We could raise and spend millions of dollars marketing online trying to reach 100,000 shoppers or we could get paid to sell our flowers to supermarkets and expose our brand to 20,000 shoppers *per store per week*. Imagine that – in 400 to 500 stores and we're reaching an audience of millions.

I put together and acquired three companies as a founding base to make this project possible. The first acquisition was an organic online floral company already selling nationwide. The second was a technology company to handle the future needs of touch screen devices in supermarkets nationwide. Again, we could spend money hiring an in-house technology team to manage our needs or acquire a company already profitable in handling its own customer base. Our IT department was a profit center, not a cost center. The third acquisition was a company called Total Floral that sold to supermarkets. We had the three pillars of a brand that could reach far and wide bringing our business model to the masses.

The next goal was to raise some capital to make acquisitions of online floral companies. Everyone was struggling against the larger online companies like 1800Flowers® and ProFlowers®. We had two very good mid-size online retailers ready to join our team. Like us, they benefited from being able to share expenses and focus more dollars on e-marketing. In the midst of our capital raise, we lost Total Floral, one of the three pillars of the business and fund raising efforts. Our largest customer at Total Floral was a 100-store supermarket chain in Florida called Sweetbay Supermarkets. Sweetbay was purchased by Winn-Dixie Supermarkets and we were thrown out just like that. Some $3.8M of our revenue was *gone* almost overnight – and this was a *huge* black eye for us as we were trying to raise capital. No one wants to invest in a company that just lost that much revenue. I spent a few years trying to pivot into a different model focused more in online retail, but since we needed to acquire and merge with other retailers, we faced growing costs and efficiency issues as a small ecommerce company. We had pressures coming from all corners due to increases in fuel, labor, and competition from Amazon and 1-800-Flowers. There was even pressure from a *Shark Tank* company – yep, the one you see on TV.

We operated an online wholesale company that sold flowers to retailers nationwide and shipped via overnight FedEx. Our company Ecoflowers.com® had been running for five years at this point and we had a registered trademark with the national trademark office. Some people in Utah decided to open a business called Ecoflower.com by dropping the *s* and selling dried flowers online. They went on *Shark Tank,* got an investment from Damon Johns, and trampled *all over* our trademark and brand. They blatantly dared us to sue them for trademark infringement knowing they could outspend me defending the suit. This company did such a poor job supplying their customers they destroyed our good name. Consumers would call threatening us when they weren't even our customers.

The Better Business Bureau gave us "F" ratings all over the country. These people were taking their customers' money in advance and not shipping to some of them for six months. There were Facebook pages titled IHateEcoflowers, which was our company and *not* the dried flower company.

I met with our Intellectual Property Lawyers to discuss the case. Because a national celebrity was involved they wanted to dig right in and take it on. First, they wanted a huge retainer from us to just *look* into the owners of the other company and find out how much backing they actually had. This not being my first legal challenge, I pushed back and said let's give it a few months and see what they do with my cease and desist letter. Being lawyers, they didn't want me reaching out directly because they always feel they are the only ones who can negotiate a deal. I find the opposite to be true. What was at stake here was we were clearly wronged, we had a registered trademark and we could sue for damages. What I've learned over the years about suing is plentiful. You pay an attorney $10K to investigate. When the money's gone they determine first if it is a credible case and for another $25k retainer they will look into it. The plan is either to intimidate the defendants into a fight or abandoning the use of your intellectual property. If they discontinue, you just spent $35k and they say "Oops, sorry our bad!"

If they have deep pockets, want to fight you, or want to move forward to sue for damages, you could get hundreds of thousands of dollars awarded by the court. Well, guess what they do? They close down and file bankruptcy. You just spend $50-$100k to get a judgment that's uncollectable. Do you know who wins? Your lawyer and theirs. It's a huge racket if you let your emotions get into it. I told my lawyer, "Let's see what happens. At the rate they are upsetting consumers, I can't see them being in business much longer. Again, what will we win if I spend all this money and they go out of business anyhow?"

Sure enough, they closed five months later. Those guys destroyed our name, but I was only out $2,000 in phone calls with a blood-thirsty attorney. Given the circumstances, I felt it was a win.

CHAPTER FIFTEEN: Haiti and Goodwill

Sometime in 2011, I was contacted by an NGO (non-governmental organization) about helping them in Haiti after the devastating earthquake in 2010. They had seen a story about some of the sunflower projects I had been working on in Ecuador where we helped small landowners grow sunflowers and export them to other countries for earning income. The goal was to help people with minimal earning potential and provide them with an opportunity to make income from their land beyond raising chickens and vegetables for local consumption.

I agreed to travel to Haiti to see the project after studying what they had already done. It was an impressive project offering free housing to Haitian people who qualified and adhered to the program of health, safety, and economic sustainability. The NGO had set up a safe space for children. Child safety was a major problem in Haiti with kids being abused or recruited into lives of prostitution or crime. They set up medical facilities for preventative treatments for program residents. The last element was recipients of these homes needed to be employed at various economic development projects set up by the NGO. One of these projects proposed by me was running a sunflower farm - products which can be exported and sold to other markets. Having done a few of these projects successfully in Ecuador, it made perfect sense for the same level of success in Haiti. Sunflowers are easy to grow, and can withstand poor soil with full sun exposure. Seeds are less than two cents each and the technical experience needed to grow sunflowers is minimal. It was something with which I could surely help.

Haiti is a beautiful country with a long history of violence and corrupt politics. The Haitians I met were mostly well educated and working restlessly to rebuild their country. These were proud men and women who gave me a historical sense of the decades and centuries of struggles. From their perspective, the U.S. had been a big brother waving a big stick, at times interfering with their elections, supporting opposition candidates, and even organizing a coup against leaders they did not like. It is not an uncommon story I hear often while traveling to foreign countries where the CIA or other operatives do the work of the Department of the State picking and supporting candidates who will be beneficial to U.S. National Security or financial interests. I'm not against it, but I find it so interesting when I see media reports of Russia or China trying to interfere in U.S. elections since the U.S. government is likely one of the larger meddlers in foreign affairs around the globe.

Haiti has been under military rule at times and democracy at others. At one point, the U.S. had sanctions against Haiti in protest of particular leaders of the country and as a result for a decade Haiti had limited trading partners in the Caribbean nations and throughout the world. When you fly around Haiti, you can clearly see the borders with the Dominican Republic. Haiti has been forced to strip its national resources to build internally and sell to the nations to which they can. As a result, the mountains on the Haiti side are stripped of trees, while the DR side is lush and tropical. The stripping of the national resources leaves Haiti susceptible to mudslides during tropical storms and hurricanes. It also leaves the country with little internal industry to power its economy.

I learned during my visit and subsequent research that Haiti was known as the NGO capital of the world and considered very corrupt. After the earthquake, many nations came to the aid of Haiti with resources for displaced Haitians. NGOs swooped in to start projects and while those behind NGOs are well-intentioned, there is a nasty backside to these organizations that revolve only around money. At the time, there were over 2,500 NGOs stationed in Haiti doing various projects. In order to be best suited to help in Haiti, one was required to deal with a certain level of corruption not unlike the flower industries in Latin America.

In order to do so, the following conditions must be met:

- Each NGO must hire x number of locals.
- There must be a lead person.
- To get US Aid you had to buy 3 vehicles from a defined Toyota dealership in Ft Lauderdale.
- Housing and offices must be rented which caused so much administrative redundancy with over 2,500 NGOs.
- Any imports such as food, medical supplies, etc. must be sold to the heads of government companies and buy them back to give them to those in need.

Some will argue this is how the economy is stimulated. I'll buy that assumption to a certain extent, but it's also a "Who's Who?" of local government leaders and donors to US politicians lining their pockets with billions in aid which was designated to get basic services to those in need. I had meetings with several of these leaders trying to work out how to develop our project within the framework of a developing nation like Haiti.

One of the most vital aspects of the project was finding land on which to grow and the local infrastructure needed to support it. We needed someone who knew how to grow the products, could manage workers effectively, and also understood refrigeration and held export experience. One of the local Haitians working for the NGO set up a meeting for me with a tomato grower outside Port-Au-Prince. It made sense because both products were perishable, agricultural items. I had a driver who showed me around the country and was introduced to me as Chaperon. His name in French was far too difficult for me to pronounce, so Chaperon had to do. On the way to the meeting, Chaperon told me the man I was about to meet had just returned from a ten-year exile in the Dominican Republic following a failed assassination attempt on the president of Haiti. This information was a little disconcerting but also sounded so much like an exaggerated tale so I didn't give it much thought other than it made a cool story.

As we got to the warehouse of the tomato farm, I realized it was a large-scale commercial operation that actually appeared abandoned. A guard came out of the massive gate doors at the entrance of the facility, took my passport, and presumably made a call to the man I was about to see. The guard returned to the car, gave back my passport, and opened the gates for us. Inside the compound, the area looked as if it was straight out of an apocalypse film. It had certainly been abandoned for ten years or more, which began to add validity to Chaperon's story.

We were signaled to drive through the open doors of a large warehouse; it was dark inside. Once inside, we were told to stop and get out. As I got out of the car, I slipped on something on the ground that seemed to roll. I shuffled my feet and heard metal being kicked around over and over. I looked down to find myself slipping on something that rolled like it had been balancing on large ball bearings. Walking under a large skylight revealed hundreds of empty 9mm casings from either a lot of semi-automatic weapons or a few fully automatic weapons. We continued to walk and eventually exited the warehouse to the outdoors. I spotted more brass everywhere, mostly 9mm but a bunch of shotgun shells as well. What the hell had I gotten myself into? I'd seen a lot of stuff in Bogota, but it appeared that there had been a recent gunfight on this property. Frankly, it was quite unsettling ground for me.

We walked toward a rusty metal staircase on the side of the warehouse and were informed our contact was upstairs in his office. As we walked up, the staircase was so rusty that parts of it had fallen through, but we made it to the top and a man gestured for us to enter. I thought to myself, *"This has to be our contact."* He was a large man in his late fifties whom I later learned was of Iranian descent but had been in Haiti since he was a child. He wore several gold chains, had a loud thunderous voice, sipped a small cup of espresso, and was smoking cigarettes one right after the other. His actions made him look like he was on the verge of a heart attack. He was on the phone when we entered so we got hand gestures to sit as he loudly expressed what I could only imagine was his frustration over something. He was one scary dude.

He got off the phone, welcomed us, and introduced himself as Jean Rene. Chaperon thanked him for taking the time to meet me and introduced me. I shook his hand and thanked him as well. Chaperon then explained what the NGO was doing in Haiti and how I was brought in for the economic development aspect of the project. I chimed in and gave him a brief background on myself, my company, and what we had done elsewhere, as well as how I would be attempting to do the same here. As I was explaining all of this to him, two younger men came in to face us, both with pistols in their waistbands.

Jean Rene introduced one as his son and the other as a bodyguard, explaining to us that Haiti had become a different place since the earthquake and security was now a major concern even for the locals. Chaperon then took this opportunity to ask Jean Rene where he had been for the past ten years and why. At this point, I found myself eager to discover the validity of Chaperon's story, but I would never have been so forward to ask.

Jean Rene proceeded to tell us he had been forced out of the country ten years prior after being tortured in front of his family in his home by the Haitian President's security detail. Chaperon asked boldly, "Did you work for the CIA, is that the reason you had to leave so suddenly?" I was shocked at what I was hearing and the brazenness of Chaperon to ask such a bold, in-depth question.

Jean Rene went on to explain, "Yes, I was…" He turned to face me, "Your CIA. As a result, the Haitian President believed I was going to assassinate him so he came for me and my family in the middle of the night."

Chaperon showed no signs of backing down and asked, "Well, was that true?"

Jean Rene agreed, " You are not wrong, but let's move on to our discussion about agriculture. At this point, I was ready to leave because it was scarier than anything I had experienced in Colombia or Ecuador. Chaperon kept pushing forward with the purpose of the visit, growing sunflowers on his land, and having him join and partner with me and my company to make it happen.

After discussing the broader strokes of a project, Jean Rene asked, "Do you want to see where we could grow them?"

I said, "Yes please," but all I wanted to do was get out of there. We walked down from the office and I asked Jean Rene, "What happened here with all these bullet shells all over the floor?"

He replied, "Don't worry about those, Robert, we were hunting doves here. Someone will pick them up." I'm not quite sure who hunts doves with a 9mm, but I suppose the 12 gauge shells I saw there could offer some truth in that regard. It just added to the creepiness of the entire visit.

Jean Rene told Chaperon to wait there, because he was going to take me in his truck to see the farm, and we would meet back up with him after. It was another of those times in my young life in which I had two options: Look stupid and scared OR risk losing your life. Yup, you guessed it. I would rather die than run away from this guy, hop in with Chaperon, and tell him to hit it. So instead, I got in the 1980 mint condition Ford Bronco and took an hour drive with Jean Rene out to the most remote former tomato fields I had ever seen. As we drove I listened with interest as he shared the history of his farms and how he was rebuilding them following his return. It was like any other tour I had gone to in any other country with any grower.

Obviously, I survived this ordeal, made it back to the warehouse, and safely into Chaperon's car. We thanked Jean Rene for his time and explained we would get back to him. On the drive back to the NGO compound, Chaperon was so excited, thinking he would be the perfect partner for us in Haiti to manage the entire sunflower project. Unlimited land, good infrastructure, and a strong partner to make things happen.

I turned to Chaperon and explained, "I'm sorry, he is not the partner for me. I have dealt with many partners in developing nations over the years on various projects. Sometimes you have disagreements with partners and sometimes you just have to sit and work things out face-to-face. I don't believe Jean Rene deals with disagreements the same way I do and I don't want to be on the opposite side of a misunderstanding with him."

I left Haiti with the agreement that I would be back in three months and we would interview more potential partners. It would give the NGO time to do a little extra groundwork and set up new meetings. By the third month, the NGO lost its major funding and was in the process of pulling out of Haiti, so we never got to plant the first seed. *"How unfortunate,"* I thought. I really felt connected to this project and the people of Haiti I had met.

Just recently as I was finishing this book, March 13, 2024, I was in Labadee, Haiti, enjoying a cruise at Royal Caribbean's private beach. Haiti had just been taken over by gangs a few weeks prior, 4,000 inmates were released from the prisons and had taken over 80 percent of Port-a-Prince and the government. The current Prime Minister was in Kenya begging for 1,000 troops to assist Haiti when the airport was taken over. He was unable to return.

Cellular service was cut while we were on the island. It was a beautiful day on the island when we received word that the next cruise ship had been diverted for safety concerns. We were the last to visit this port. All future cruises were being diverted and Royal was not booking any more Labadee stops until the fall of 2024. Haiti, always with the drama – those poor people. I'll be back when it clears up.

CHAPTER SIXTEEN: New Consulting Projects and High Altitudes

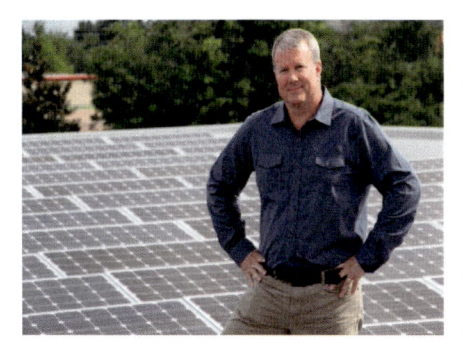

As we began winding down the online business from all these challenges, I was back consulting for various businesses. In addition to flower companies, I consulted for Goodwill Industries of Central Florida while serving as their Chief Sustainability Officer. I helped them raise money to put solar panels on their retail locations. The project generated more than 80 percent of the stores' daily power needs. Negotiating with solar companies was an exciting project, as was setting up fundraising campaigns and securing grant money to fund the project.

At one point, I put together a program called Sunflowers for Good in which we partnered with the University of Florida Agriculture extension near Orlando International Airport. We grew five acres of sunflowers for sale to wholesalers and supermarkets. The proceeds went to store solar panel funding.

During this time I started a consulting project with a potted plant grower in Florida on the Gulf Coast. They had some e-marketing needs and ironically my family was from the area. I had recently inherited a home after my mother's passing, so I had a place to stay and focus on the needs of this company. Over time, as many consulting projects do, it grew into more of a please help manage my business project. The company, founded in 1892, was once one of the largest cut flower growers in the country.

After spending the 80s and 90s in South America helping growers convert from traditional to sustainable production and meeting the volume needs of supermarkets nationwide I was now part of an example of growers that couldn't compete with growers down south. The company had shut down its cut flower business but still had a potted plant farm and wholesale floral business. Land development had become the owners' main focus.

Visiting South America over the years always included growers who "know a guy that knows a guy that wants to sell his products in North America." I've had packages left for me at the front desk, notes slipped under my hotel room door, and people waiting in the lobby to catch me on the way in or out. I'd love to think I'm just that awesome but this is common practice. They love to make a deal and have the work ethic to make it happen.

I've visited broccoli, potato, strawberry, hearts of palm, honey, horses, sheep, pigs, and organic dairy farms just to name a few. I've even toured a baby food company in Bolivia because a flower grower's wife had a factory. Another grower flew me down to the country to look at his onion farm.

I had a national retailer ask me to find the best quinoa available so I did – in Bolivia. Bolivia is an interesting country and they grow the best quality quinoa high in the Andes Mountains. I've visited high in the Andes for years. Ecuador's capital is at 9,000 feet and some of the farms surrounding it are 10,000 or higher. Bolivia's capital, La Paz will test your ability to handle high altitudes from the first day until you depart.

At 12,000 feet above sea level it is the world's highest major city. From the moment you get off the plane and walk 20 paces you feel it. On the long walk to immigration, there are Oxygen Stations for tourists and the elderly who may not be able to make the walk. Hypoxia can happen at 8,000 feet and 12,000 feet made for a very uncomfortable week. While the city is at 12,000 feet most of my meetings were up in the highlands at 14,000 which is equal to the summit of Mt. Rainier in Washington State.

Going into Bolivia and coming from Florida's sea level, I tried to acclimate by going to Bogota first. Because of flight cancellations I diverted to Lima, Peru, which is on the coast at sea level. Not exactly going to help me adjust. Bolivians and tourists drink tea made from coca leaves (the main ingredient in cocaine). It is supposed to assist with altitude sickness.

They also have pills to help, called *Sorojchi*. These are two things I had vowed I would never take. By day three, my head was pounding and my legs were aching and I was ready for anything. The tea was available in the hotel so I ordered some. Next up were the *Sorojchi* pills which people were offering me at every meeting. I'm not sure whether these things worked or if they only slowed the debilitating pains at every meeting and the sleepless nights. I'd been to 14,000 feet before but living and working there day and night became a real challenge.

Like most South American countries, there were riots going on to make things even more difficult. Tires burning in the streets and roads blocked off. We spent days taking detours and dodging roadblocks to get where we needed to go. Needless to say, this was a week I was ready to be over.

As I settled into my first class seat to head home, I could see into the cockpit where the pilots were wearing oxygen masks. Not only was I jealous but I was concerned after speaking to the flight attendant who explained the FAA requires pilots to wear oxygen when departing an airport at this altitude. I googled what the equivalent altitude was inside a pressurized cabin. It is the equivalent of 8,000 feet so I was anxiously waiting to take off to get some relief. Sure enough an hour into my flight the headache was gone and I fell into a deep sleep dreaming of the Florida humidity at sea level where I could hike miles and sleep soundly.

The same year I went looking for the perfect cup of coffee in the Coffee Triangle of Colombia. This rich growing area of

Colombia is between three main cities – Bogota, Medellin and Cali. It is a rich fertile growing region for many crops, some not so legal. While it's not the safest place to visit without knowing where you are going, I had a grower from the flower industry who also exported coffee to take me into the wild for a firsthand look at the world-renowned coffee farms and the artisan sugar industry. In Colombia, they use natural sugar in their coffee known as *Panela*.

Panela is raw sugar cane juice which has been cooked down via a method that's been around for hundreds of years in Colombia as opposed to the more modern method of factory processing though a centrifuge. The cover of this book is from one of those farms where the cane was brought in from the field on burros. While I was looking to learn more about the coffee industry, I was specifically looking for shade grown coffee which has more flavor than commercially grown field coffees that trade as futures on stock exchanges worldwide. We drove deep into the canopies of the rainforest looking for coffee and as expected we found a dense lush section of plants on the side of the mountain. We climbed out of the truck, slid down a few steep cliffs and cut our way through the tall grasses until we started to see these plants full of lush green leaves. Peering through the dense forest we began to hear voices and then what resembled a makeshift warehouse came into view. The coffee grower who was from a nearby plantation and acting as my guide grabbed me and signaled me quietly to quickly follow him back to our truck. We had quite the climb back. The high altitude and the steep climb had my heart racing. I knew what he was going to tell me when we got back to the truck. It was not a coffee packing warehouse in the jungle we had stumbled upon but a cocaine factory. We had found a product made in Colombia but not the coffee I was looking for! We drove back up and down two mountain tops to the area in which we started. Rains can be very dangerous on these trails through the jungle and it began to pour down. We could see the trail ahead of us was quite steep and a river of water was rolling down. The farm owner driving us around knew exactly where to go, the house of a lady who worked in his coffee plantation. She was a very sweet older lady who welcomed us into her humble home to escape the rains and for what has been the most perfect cup of coffee I ever had.

Her home barely had doors and consisted of two rooms – a bedroom and a kitchen. She had a bag of green coffee beans yet to be roasted as she began making us the most authentic cup of coffee ever. Her stove was powered by wood, so she started the stove with a few pieces of scrap lumber, which looked like pieces of a 2x4 or part of a wooden shipping pallet. The heat became intense very quickly and it felt good against the soaking we received making our way from the truck to her home. She had an iron skillet on top of the stove. She shaved from a block of Panela the right amount of sugar into the pan in which she roasted the raw coffee beans. She continued the roast, adding more beans or shaving off more Panela until every bean was roasted darker than any espresso bean I had seen and was infused with raw sugar cane juices. After letting the beans cool, she communicated with the grower to get her grinder from the next room. He came out with a traditional grinder like one would see in a flea market but never in any modern kitchen today. We took her kitchen table, flipped it on its end, and mounted the grinder with its clamp on the side of the table. We took turns feeding in the beans and cranking the grinder into a ceramic plate. We now had a mountain of freshly roasted and ground coffee that smelled like nothing I had ever experienced from popping open a can of Maxwell House. I now wondered how she was going to brew it, I knew she didn't have a Mr. Coffee behind the wood pile or this dream would be over. Of course not –

she put it in a pot, poured bottled water over it, and brewed it on the stove.

Now, I have tried to make campfire coffee before on my various hiking trips and always ended up with dirty coffee water and a mouth full of grounds so I was a little disappointed and almost began to wish she did have a Mr. Coffee. I was wrong again, she made the perfect cup of coffee without a single grain of coffee from the first sip to the last drop. I realized I just had the perfect cup of coffee and there is no cruise ship excursion that could ever buy this kind of experience no matter the price. It took me at least three years after that trip to realize I would never make a cup as good as she did, and it was time for me to move on knowing the pinnacle of my coffee experience had been reached.

When I arrived home from the trip I asked the grower to send me a sample box of his coffee so I could test it. Instead of shipping it FedEx or DHL like we would do here in the U.S. He gave it to an airline stewardess to put in her carry-on bag, then shipped it to me from Miami. It came wrapped up in cellophane like a brick of cocaine, obviously someone in his shipping department used to work for you know who. I received three bricks in three different shipments over the course of a few weeks. Colombians are always unique and surprising – you never know what you're going to get.

CHAPTER SEVENTEEN: Climbing to New Heights - Mexico

Years of trips to South America gave me hours of gazing out the window passing over the Jungles and rainforests of that beautiful continent. Sometimes I would daydream of hiking through those jungles. Others I would spend asking myself if we crash, what is my plan and exit from such a vast, inhospitable place? These thoughts sparked my interest in hiking and mountain climbing. Ecuador is known as the avenue of the volcanos and I've always told myself one day I would climb Mt. Cotopaxi, south of Ecuador's capital.

I've passed this snow capped volcano 100 times while visiting farms in the area. In 2021, not intending to climb or summit, I walked up to over 14,000 feet of its 19,000+ peak. There were high winds and extreme cold that day, but it is something I hope to try again in the coming years. I've climbed Rainier, Baker, and Nevado de Toluca in Mexico, all four facing poor weather conditions to summit. My last visit to Mt. Rainier, in September 2020, was met with 95 mph winds at the summit that resulted in the death of one climber that day. In 2025, I have a planned 2nd attempt to summit Mt. Rainier. Let's hope the second time's the charm.

In 2020, I made the trip to climb Nevado de Toluca which is located about 100 miles from the capital of Mexico City. I flew into Mexico City, rented a car, and headed out into an area infested with drug traffickers and farms that grow flowers and marijuana among other things. The drug war in Mexico I find very different from my experiences in Colombia. Mexico is a huge distributor of drugs coming from other sources but they are always looking to take over farms of legitimate crops and force them to hide drugs in their shipments.

I had made a few farm meetings while I contemplated when and how I was going to summit this mountain another 40-50 miles outside of Toluca. The reason for my farm visits was to find support from growers that could get their products to the Port of Tuxpan where I had a ship ready to take a container to the Port of Manatee in Florida where I was consulting for a floral wholesaler. It was going to be the first shipment of flowers by boat from Mexico to the U.S. ever – another feather in my cap – and a huge savings in cost as well as a 30 times reduction in carbon output from traditional floral distribution. After two years of negotiations between ship lines, USDA inspectors, ports, growers, and customers for this much product, we received the first ship into the Port of Manatee in Florida.

I had pleaded with the ship line to allow me to camp in my tent on the cargo hold of the ship on its way over as it was a three-day voyage and I wanted to experience it firsthand. I'd once taken a cargo flight from Colombia with a load of flowers and when I say Sense of Source, I really mean I want to know it all. The cargo ship insurance company and Covid restrictions would not let me make the trip but it was still a great accomplishment. The shipment met all the requirements I had set out as a proof of concept, it was cheaper, faster, and 30 times less carbon output, plus the quality of the flowers were perfect. After three months of trying to schedule the next shipments I finally had to give in as the Covid pandemic blitz was in full force. With so many Chinese ships sitting off both coasts of the U.S. waiting to get in, the Mexican ship line I found was overbooked month after month with no end in sight. Mexico had become a huge supply of everything from kitchen appliances to medical supplies and refrigerated containers for flowers just lost priority status.

But, back to Nevado de Toluca mountain, I had finished a few days of meetings and had one afternoon to climb this mountain before returning to Mexico City and boarding my flight home. I left early in the morning, navigating my way by both map and phone GPS when my cell coverage dropped 30 minutes into my drive. I found myself in no man's land, so getting lost or getting help if needed would come at the mercy of my poor Spanish and some good hearted locals. I remember making a turn off the main road onto a dirt road at the foothills of Nevado, where I saw two military trucks with soldiers unloading sandbags. I thought to myself, *"Well this is interesting there must be a flood or one expected and they are preparing."*

I made my way to the foot of the mountain and parked the car in a place I felt it wouldn't be seen, I certainly didn't need it stolen and didn't know who might have seen me turn off the main road. This was Mexico and I wasn't going to be walking to the nearest town in hopes of help from possibly the very same people wearing my clothes and driving my car.

Nevado de Toluca is a stratovolcano but it's only 15,000 feet at the summit with no glaciers making it easier to climb than others I've attempted. I grabbed my pack and dropped in around 8,000 feet so if all went well this would be five to six hours at most to summit and return. After about two hours of hiking up around 10,000 feet I came to an upper peak trailhead with a park ranger booth. I'm not even sure how they got there. Strange to see, yes, but it's not unheard of to have to buy a permit to climb, especially since they have to come get you if something goes wrong. After five minutes of English to Spanish along with hand gestures and frustration – they keep pointing to this sign. Argh, are you serious? I'm foiled by Covid AGAIN? The mountain was closed at higher elevations because they didn't have the staff to support a rescue.

After my climb, as I drove back down, I found the military group fully set up and hiding behind the sandbags with rifles and a fully automatic weapon on a tripod. This was a drug stop location with the high risk of a shootout with cartel members not preparation for a flood. It was like being back in Colombia except I wasn't expecting this to be a hot area. It's not somewhere I would take the family but it wasn't somewhere I was concerned to be either, until then. I'm getting too old to wander into areas I really don't need to be or understand.

CHAPTER EIGHTEEN: COVID and Migration to Orlando

Covid brought many opportunities and many challenges. Despite stimulus and government assistance like PPP (paycheck protection program), companies struggled with first being shut down by their government followed by a period of customer closings, it was hard to get supply and staff. It was truly a remarkable time. I found myself trapped on the west coast of Florida having moved there temporarily for a three-year contract with a plant grower and flower wholesaler.

When Covid hit they decided to close the wholesale side of the business and cancel my contract two years early. It was not the time to find another consulting project in the difficulties of this new Covid world. And there was no way to get back to Orlando where we had lived since the early 1980s. My only option was to buy the wholesale side of the company as they closed it and muscle through the challenges of customers that were still shut down and retailers that couldn't pay past invoices as they slowly came back into business.

From there I could start to find a way back home in Orlando. From the ashes of Covid-19 with 90 percent sales declines, we set out to grow the business back to what it once was and save the jobs of as many people as possible. The first task was to increase revenue from new business channels that were growing instead of shrinking. The first 25 years of my career focused on selling to supermarkets so I knew this could potentially offset the loss of the wholesale business with just one small chain, and when the wholesale business returned as Covid-19 let up, we would have a solid business. It worked as far as getting the business back up off the ground. Now on to Orlando, we needed to open a branch in Orlando if we were to get home. I knew a company in Orlando with whom I had consulted before. It was an event business still reeling from massive loss of business brought on by Covid. I offered to rent space for our new Orlando branch but instead he offered a trade of consulting services in exchange.

After a few months an opportunity presented itself, the owner wanted to sell his company in Orlando. It was the defining break my wife and I needed - to be back in Orlando full time where our children returned after college and were beginning to settle in and getting married.

This covid time period and getting back to Orlando was the start of an entirely new story which I will save for another time - moving, living in an apartment, recovering from ransomware, a bad partner, and moving the business not once but four times as commercial real estate in the post-Covid world introduced chaos. We are now one of the leading floral and event decor companies in Orlando doing events from the Bahamas to the Carolinas. Our entrance into the theme park world has begun a new chapter where 40 years of experience has come together with a team of young professionals and our adult children poised to make this part of their story in the years to come.

If the age of people running for president in 2024 is any indicator of how old I will be when I stop working, it would appear I have several more chapters to come in my journey but they are best saved for another time. The industry today is run by large corporations with private equity partners. A small group of the largest farms own the majority of the market with the regional players diminished greatly. Whether it is a good thing or not, I'm not sure as I can make an argument for both. Even so, it is clear that the realities behind the perceptions of the sources are more blurred than ever.

Everything has a source. I hope this gives you a sense of mine and the industry I've grown to love. If you are in this business - from growing flowers on the Equator to putting the finishing touches on the most exquisite events in a resort ballroom near you – I hope you enjoyed reading about one small player in a global marketplace we all enjoy.

to be continued…………

Follow us on Facebook at Sense of Source for additional pictures and stories.

Thank you for reading,

Robert

Made in the USA
Columbia, SC
29 April 2024

b27c038a-95ee-4af6-981a-e8954487ec16R01